TIME AND MAN

Georgios I. Mantzaridis

Time and Man

Translated from the original Greek
by Julian Vulliamy
Edited by Harry Boosalis

ST. TIKHON'S SEMINARY PRESS
South Canaan, Pennsylvania 18459
1996

TIME AND MAN
Originally published in Greek by Ekdoseis P. Pournara in Thessaloniki, Greece, with the title *Chronos kai anthropos*. ©1992 by Georgios I. Mantzaridis. All rights reserved.
English translation ©1995 by St. Tikhon's Seminary Press. All rights reserved.
Cover design layout by Christopher Stanton.

Published by
ST. TIKHON'S SEMINARY PRESS
Box B
South Canaan, PA 18459 USA

Second Printing 2014
Printed in the United States of America.

Library of Congress Cataloging-in-Publication Data

Mantzarides, Georgios I.
   [Chronos kai anthropos. English]
   Time and man / Georgios I. Mantzaridis ; translated from the original Greek by Julian Vulliamy.
      p. cm.
   Includes bibliographical references and index.
   ISBN 978-0-9884574-9-2
   1. Time--Religious aspects--Christianity. 2. Man (Christian theology) 3. Orthodox Eastern Church--Doctrines. 4. Orthodox Eastern Church--Liturgy. I. Title.
BX323.M24413   1996
231.7--dc20   96-11015
                                                                                              CIP

Table of Contents

Preface .... *vii*

Translator's note .... *viii*

1. On the Problem of Time 1

2. Time and Space 15

3. Time and Life 23

4. Christ and Time 39

5. Church and Time 51

6. The Diachronic Tradition 60

7. Monasticism and the Church:
   Biological Discontinuity and Spiritual Continuity 70

8. The Transfiguration of Time 77

9. Liturgical Time 87

Epilogue 107

Index 110

Preface

The minds of not only scientists and artists but also those of common laymen have always been occupied, and continue to be keenly exercised, by the notion of time. This is only natural, since the whole of man's life and existence are governed by time. Time governs nature and the whole of the cosmos. It even governs man's every concept and understanding of the cosmos.

The cosmos exists in time. Man is born, evolves and eventually vanishes within the confines of time, yet simultaneously, time remains incomprehensible and impenetrable to man. Everyone considers it familiar and self-explanatory, yet no one has managed to explain it or describe its nature.

Time reveals the truth of man's life and this truth goes together with the state of decay and death. Without the realization and acceptance of this state, man remains estranged from the truth of life and his existence.

The question of man's correct orientation in life is, in fact, a question of his correct orientation in time; and correct orientation in time presupposes a moving towards, and an examination of, the possibilities and perspectives afforded by time.

GEORGIOS I. MANTZARIDIS

Translator's Note

All quotations from ancient and patristic texts are my own translations except where indicated in the text, and for the following:

Aristotle, *Physics*, translated by R. P. Hardie and R. K. Gaye (Oxford University Press).

Plato, *Timaeus*, translated by B. Jowett (Oxford University Press).

Plotinus, *Enneads*, translated by H. Armstrong (Loeb Classical Library).

St. Augustine, *Confessions*, translated by R. S. Pine-Coffin (Penguin).

All quotations from Scripture are from the Authorized (King James) Version.

Chapter One
On the Problem of Time

Man tends to see time as a factor in life that needs no explanation, and thinks that he knows what it is. But when he happens to ask questions about the nature of time, and tries to define it, he becomes aware of his own ignorance and inability to do so. This happens not only on an individual, but also on a universal level. The ancient Greeks took time for granted as something self-evident, without concerning themselves greatly with its nature. The Pre-Socratic philosophers, when they refer to time, do not go into a detailed investigation and analysis of it. But when speculation started as to the real nature of time, men realized that they were confronted by an impasse in their attempts to define it—an impasse that continues to exist in our day.

In the ancient Greek world, as in the world in general—apart from that of the Bible—it was the cyclical view of time that prevailed. This view is closely connected with cosmology, and especially with the acceptance of the idea of the perpetuity of matter. According to this view, the cosmos neither sets out from a particular starting point, nor does it make its way to a particular finishing point, so that in the final analysis there is no real doctrine either of protology (the first things), or of eschatology (the last things). The beginning coincides with the end, and the end is a new beginning. Time is a circle, and like a circle, it is self-contained. Everything comes back on itself or is recycled. History repeats itself. The only distinction to be made here is that some (like the Pythagoreans) held that on recycling, things return exactly as they were, while others (like Heraclitus, Empedocles and others) held that the old is destroyed and something new replaces it.

Plato regards time as being a moving image of eternity: "Wherefore he [the Creator] resolved to have a moving image of eternity, and when he set in order the heavens, he made this image eternal but moving according to number, while eternity itself rests in unity, and this image we call time."[1] Time, observes Plato, did not always exist, but was created together with the heavens. Thus, if the heavens were ever to be dissolved, then time would perish with them.[2] Time moves in circles and is expressed in numbers.[3] With Plato, the preliminary era of theorizing about time draws to a close, to be succeeded by Aristotle's systematic investigation which came to influence all later thinking on the subject.

Aristotle's first undertaking in his investigation of time is to attempt to ascertain whether or not it actually exists: "Does it belong to the class of things that exist, or to that of things that do not exist?"[4] He seems to think that it does not in fact exist. Indeed, time is the sum of two non-existent parts: the past, which "has been and no longer is," and the future which "is about to be but is not yet."[5] But the sum of two non-existent parts is also itself non-existent.

Of course, apart from the past and the future, there is also the present, or the 'now'. But the 'now', which has somehow come to be regarded as the third element of time, should not, according to Aristotle, be thought of as time at all, because if it were to be, it too should have past, present and future. The 'now' is that timeless moment through which the future passes in order to become the past.

What then is time and what is its nature?

In his quest for an answer to this question in the earlier philosophical tradition, Aristotle makes the observation that

---

[1] *Timaeus*, 37d.
[2] Ibid., 38b.
[3] Ibid., 38a.
[4] *Physics*, IV 9,217b 31.
[5] Ibid., IV 9, 217b 33-34.

On the Problem of Time

the only view worthy of consideration is that of Plato, according to which time is movement. But he goes on to say that time, although it is associated with movement, cannot be identified with it. He points out succinctly that "time is neither movement, nor is it independent of movement."[6] We perceive movement and time together, or, to put it another way, we cannot perceive time without movement. But movement has to be understood not only as change of position within space, but as any change. Thus, a mental change can also give the sense of time.[7] In this way, Aristotle also stresses the idea of so-called 'psychological time' which has been developed in the patristic tradition and in modern philosophical thought.

Just as every movement creates the sensation of time, so every sensation of time creates the sense of movement. And since time cannot be identified with movement, it has to be regarded as a *property* of movement. Aristotle eventually comes to the conclusion that time is "number of motion in respect of 'before' and 'after'."[8] And since the word *number* can mean both that which is counted and that with which we count, Aristotle makes it clear that time is "that which is counted and not that with which we count."[9] The various different movements and durations of time are integrated into the 'now'. The 'now' is neither time nor even a particle of time, but a timeless incision into time. If Aristotle had been acquainted with differential calculus, it would perhaps have been possible for him to see the 'now' and its position in time from another point of view. Nevertheless, he does not omit to point out that neither could the 'now' be understood without time, nor time without the 'now'.[10]

---

[6] Ibid., IV 11, 219a 1.

[7] "For even when it is dark and we are not being affected through the body, if any movement takes place in the mind we at once suppose that some time also elapsed." Ibid., 219a 4-6.

[8] Ibid., 219b 1-2.

[9] Ibid., 219b 8.

[10] "Clearly too, if there were no time, there would be no 'now', and vice versa. Just as the moving body and its locomotion involve each other mutually, so too do the number of the moving body and the number of its

Aristotle observes that time is the cause of decay. And it is the cause of decay because it is the number of change. But "change removes what is,"[11] that is, it removes that which is from its existence. Thus, all perishable beings exist in time. And time exists because the soul exists which can measure that which measures. Thus time is an expression of the soul of man.[12]

Finally, as well as the concept of time, Aristotle also employs the concept of *kairos*. *Kairos* is the opportune time for something.[13] For every thing there is usually an opportune moment, a *kairos*. However, time itself has no *kairos*, since we are not waiting for something which will reveal the meaning of time, for the highest good is to be found beyond time.

The Neo-Platonists, like Plato, associate time with eternity. Plotinus in particular, who lived in the third century A.D. and was a contemporary of Origen, states that no one can understand time unless he takes eternity as his point of departure, since, as Plato has said, time is the image of eternity.[14] Eternity is "life at rest."[15] Time, which is the image of eternity, is related to it in the same way that the sensible is related to the intelligible. Instead of intelligible life, there is another life, which corresponds to it, the life of the soul of the world, where time exists. Time does not have its origins outside the soul of the world, just as eternity does not have its origins outside being.[16]

The biblical view of time is different. In the Old Testament, time is identified with its content. There is no concept here of time as an absolute on which the events of history are to be recorded, but it is the events themselves and their unfolding that are the constituents of time. The events are not intelligible without time, and time is not intelligible without the events.[17] Moreover, belief in the creation of the cosmos from

---

locomotion." Ibid., 219b 33-220a 3.

[11]Ibid., IV 12, 221b 3 (trans. by Hardie and Gaye, Oxford University Press).

[12]Ibid., IV 14, 223a 16 ff.

[13]*Nicomachean Ethics* I, 4, 1096a 23-27.

[14]" . . . for when we know that which holds the position of archetype, it will perhaps become clear how it is with its image, which the philosophers say time is." Plotinus, *Enneads* 3,7,1.

[15]Ibid., 3,7,11.

[16]Ibid.

[17]See G. von Rad, *Theologie des Alten Testaments*, vol. 2, München 1965,

nothing, which is unknown in ancient Greek thought, and the expectation of the fulfillment of the promises of God to his chosen people within history, dictate the adoption of a linear concept of time. The cosmos has a beginning and is heading for an end. God, who is the Creator and Lord of the cosmos, is also the Lord of time and of history. He chooses his people, he walks with them, manifests himself in history, helps his people, guides them and steers them towards the fulfillment of his promises to them.

With the coming of Christ, and his presence in the world, a new perspective is introduced into time. The *eschaton* (the end) is offered to us in the present, and every moment in history assumes an eschatological character.[18] While for Israel, interest centered on the saving revelations of time and history, in the Church, time and history are orientated towards eternity. Christ is the fulfillment of the Law and the Prophets. In his person are fulfilled God's promises to his chosen people.[19] And this fulfillment lays the foundations for the final promise of eternal life. In his life and his teaching, in his Death and Resurrection, Christ gave to man the prospect of eternity. It is this new perspective that imbues the New Testament and the whole of the Church's tradition.

Of particular interest in the examination of the Church's understanding of time is St. Basil the Great's teaching on the subject. St. Basil did not, of course, write any systematic study on the subject of time, but in his commentary on Scripture, and especially in the *Hexaemeron*, and also in his refutation of Eunomios's heretical ideas about the person of Christ, he spoke frequently about time and put forward important arguments which have enriched the Church's literature.[20]

Time, observes St. Basil, is "that space which is co-extensive with the foundation of the world."[21] Time is organically linked

---

(4th ed.) p. 108 ff. for more on this subject.

[18]See, e.g. John 5:25.

[19]Luke 4:21.

[20]The main texts for Basil's teaching on this subject are the following: *Hexaemeron* (chiefly Homilies 1 and 2), *On the Holy Spirit*, and *Against Eunomios*.

[21]*Against Eunomios* 1,21, PG29, 560B.

with space and cannot be understood without it. Its creation was instantaneous. In other words, both time and space were created timelessly by the will of God. St. Basil also understands the phrase "In the beginning God created the heaven and the earth"[22] in the same way. Just as the beginning of the road, he points out, is not yet a road, and the beginning of the house is not a house, in the same way also the beginning of time is not yet time, nor even part of time. If someone maintains that the beginning is time too, then he must also be able to divide it into beginning, middle and end, and this cannot be done.[23]

The linear passage of time contains never-ending cycles of time which are an image of eternity,[24] and impart a spiral form to time. Moreover, the march of time is intrinsic to the world and the things of the world. It accompanies them constantly, with no interruption. Reminding us of Aristotle's arguments for the three dimensions of time, St. Basil asks: "Is not time like this, that the past has vanished, the future is not yet with us, and the present, before we realize it, escapes our perception of it?"[25] Thus everything that exists within space and time is fluid and perishable. The nature of time is proper to the perishable nature of the cosmos.[26]

Apart from time, there is also the 'aeon', or the 'eternal'. As we have seen, Plato saw time as being a moving image of the 'eternal'. But in Christian literature, the concept of the 'eternal' is secondary and subordinate to a third idea, that of the 'aidion',[27] or the 'everlasting'. This change is dictated by the

---

[22]Gen. 1:1.

[23]*Hexaemeron* 1,6, PG29, 16C-17A.

[24]See *On the Holy Spirit* 27,66, PG32, 189B ff. For more on the subject see D. Tsamis, *I Protologia tou Megalou Vasiliou*, Thessaloniki 1970, p. 53ff.

[25]*Hexaemeron* 1,5, PG29, 13B.

[26]"It is therefore fit that the bodies of animals and plants, obliged to follow a sort of current and carried away by the motion which leads them to birth or death, should live in the midst of surroundings whose nature is in accord with being subject to change." Basil, *Hexaemeron* 1,5, PG29, 13C.

[27]Cf. Origen, *De Principiis* 1,8,4. For more on the understanding of time in Origen see P. Tjamalikos's interesting book, *The Concept of Time in Origen*, Berne 1991.

theological presuppositions of Christianity, which did not exist in the ancient Greek world. In Christian theology we have the distinction not only between the visible and the invisible world, but also the even more fundamental distinction between, on the one hand, the uncreated God, and on the other, the created world, which is divided into the visible and the invisible. 'Eternity' does not constitute a completely timeless state, but was created along with the spiritual world and coexists with it without end. So that just as time is intrinsic to the world perceived by the senses, so 'eternity' too is intrinsic to the created world of the spirit. Finally, the Day of the Lord, or the eighth day is also described as 'eternal' because it represents the state of the world to come.[28]

The third, and loftiest concept is that of the 'aidion',* or the 'everlasting', which is a concept peculiar to the uncreated and timeless God. The superiority of the everlasting over the eternal is incomparably greater than that of the eternal over the temporal. And this is only natural, since time and eternity are associated with the created world, whether sensible or supersensible, while the everlasting belongs to the uncreated and pre-eternal God. The everlasting, says St. Basil, is that which is "older than all time and eternity in its being."[29] And since the everlasting surpasses the created, that is why it is incomprehensible to the world.

St. Gregory the Theologian makes the observation that man lives and thinks within time, and for this reason is unable to comprehend and describe the things that are beyond time. Thus, when he refers to the generation of the Son or to the

---

*Translator's note: The usual translation of the Greek word *aidion* as 'everlasting' is not strictly accurate. Literally, it means 'always (*aei*) the same (*idion*)' and 'ever-existent' would perhaps be a better translation, since it refers specifically to uncreated 'time'. I have nevertheless retained the conventional 'everlasting' as being less cumbersome.

---

[28]"This day without evening, without succession and without end, is not unknown to Scripture, and it is the day that the Psalmist calls the eighth day, because it is outside this time of weeks. Thus whether you call it day, or whether you call it eternity, you express the same idea." Basil, *Hexaemeron* 2,8, PG28, 182D-184A.

[29]*Against Eunomios*, 2,17, PG29,608C.

procession of the Holy Spirit, the expressions he uses prove inadequate because they are associated with time.[30] The Son and the Holy Spirit, although they proceed from the Father, are 'co-everlasting' as he is. The linking of the generation of the Son or the procession of the Spirit with any idea of time is improper: "for those things which are the origin of time cannot be subject to time."[31] But even time itself remains incomprehensible to man: "Does time fall within time, or is it to be reckoned as being outside time? And if it is thought to fall within time, then within what time? And what function does this time have apart from the other? And how does it contain time? If, on the other hand, it is not thought to fall within time, what is this prodigious wisdom that introduces timeless time?"[32]

St. Gregory of Nyssa stresses the tremendous difference that exists between created and uncreated nature and notes that the former is limited by both time and space, while the latter transcends any notion of limitation.[33] Human life unfolds 'in space', beginning at some starting point and proceeding to some finishing point. Thus, it falls naturally into two distinct parts: that part which is already over and remains in the memory, and that part which is still awaited and represents the object of our hope.[34] But participation in divine life offers the man of faith the possibility of a constant reaching forward,[35] so

---

[30]"Put another question and I will answer it. Since when has the Son been begotten? Since as long as the Father has not been begotten. Since when has the Spirit been proceeding? Since as long as the Son has not been proceeding but being begotten in a nontemporal way that transcends explanation. We cannot, though, explain the meaning of 'supra-temporal' and deliberately keep clear of any suggestion of time. Expressions like 'when', 'before x', 'after y', and 'from the beginning', are not free from temporal implications, however much we try to wrest them. No, we cannot explain it, except possibly by taking the world-era as the period coinciding with eternal things, being a period which is not, as 'time' is, measured and fragmented by the Sun's motion." Gregory the Theologian, *Theological Orations* 3(29), 3, PG36, 77A.

[31]Ibid.

[32]Ibid., 3,9 PG36, 85B.

[33]*Against Eunomios* 12, PG45,933A.

[34]Ibid., 1064C.

[35]"But it is always so, that what is good now, however great and perfect it

that he increases constantly in that which is good as he participates in that which is unfailing and everlasting.[36]

According to St. Maximos the Confessor, time is "circumscribed movement,"[37] which is measured from the creation of the world. If the world did not exist, then neither would time. Time is the measure of those things which are sensible, while eternity is the measure of those things which are intelligible.[38] Eternity is time stood still. Time is eternity in motion.[39] The common feature of all things is their created nature. God, on the other hand, who is the Creator of all things, is uncreated and beyond time and eternity which define the nature of created beings.[40] Man's nature unfolds in time and is subject to change. But when it is united to God, it becomes released from that subjection to change induced by time, and acquires a state of ever-changing stillness, or still perpetual-motion.[41] Union with God does not put an end to the created nature of man, but joins it to the uncreated grace of God. Man becomes what God is, "without sharing his essence."[42] He becomes, in the words of St. Maximos, "without beginning and without end, no longer bearing within him that life that changes with time, that has a beginning and an end, and is rocked by much suffering, but rather possessing only the divine life imparted by the indwelling Word of God, that is everlasting and not limited by any form of death."[43]

---

seems to be, is only the beginning of what lies beyond it and is greater still. So that there is truth in that apostolic expression about forever reaching forward to what lies beyond, while remaining oblivious to what has already been accomplished." *On the Song of Songs* 6, PG44,885D–888A.

[36]Gregory of Nyssa, op.cit., PG44,940D-941A.
[37]*Various Texts*, 5,47, PG90, 1368C.
[38]"The measure of beings is as follows: eternity is the measure of intelligible things, and time of sensible things." *Commentary on 'On the Divine Names' of St. Dionysios the Areopagite* 5,8, PG4,336AB.
[39]"For eternity is time when it stops moving, and time is eternity when it is measured as it is borne by movement, so that I arrive at the all-embracing definition of eternity as being time deprived of movement, and time as eternity measured by movement." *De Ambiguis*, PG91,1164BC.
[40]*De Ambiguis*, PG91, 1153AB.
[41]See *To Thalassios*, PG90,760A. *Various Texts*, 5,48, PG90, 1368D-1369A.
[42]*De Ambiguis*, PG91, 1308B.
[43]*De Ambiguis*, PG91, 144C.

The eternal of itself is not without beginning. But frequently the idea of the eternal is also used with reference to God, in which case it also includes the meaning of having no beginning. In this case the eternal becomes synonymous with the everlasting. St. John Damascene, in summarizing earlier patristic tradition, observes that the term eternal ('aeon') has many different meanings. It is the name given to the span of a man's life, it is the term used to denote the entirety of our life in this world or in the world to come, and it also means that which transcends time and is coextensive with those things which are intelligible.[44] Thus God too is called eternal, but because he is also the Creator of the ages, he is also called pre-eternal. He alone is without beginning and Creator of all ages and all things that exist.[45]

Later Christian tradition sees time from the perspective that we have already presented. But of special importance in this tradition are the arguments of St. Augustine, who made his mark on the whole of later Christian thought in the West.

St. Augustine addresses himself to God in his efforts to analyze the meaning of time, and says: "It is therefore true to say that when you had not made anything, there was no time, because time itself was of your making. And no time is co-eternal with you, because you never change; whereas, if time never changed, it would not be time. What, then, is time? There can be no quick and easy answer, for it is no simple matter even to understand what it is, let alone find words to explain it. Yet, in our conversation, no word is more familiarly used or more easily recognized than 'time'. We certainly understand what is meant by the word both when we use it ourselves and when we hear it used by others. What, then, is time? I know well enough what it is, provided that nobody asks me; but if I am asked what it is and try to explain, I am baffled.

---

[44]"For what time is to those things that are under the rule of time, eternity is to those things which are everlasting." *Exposition of the Orthodox Faith*, 2,1(15), PG94,864. It is particularly characteristic here of John Damascene that he uses the idea of the 'everlasting' as being synonymous with the idea of the 'eternal'.

[45]Ibid.

On the Problem of Time

All the same I can confidently say that I know that if nothing passed, there would be no past time; if nothing were going to happen, there would be no future time; and if nothing *were*, there would be no present time."[46]

St. Augustine goes on to ask: "Of these three divisions of time, then, how can two, the past and the future, *be*, when the past no longer is and the future is not yet? As for the present, if it were always present and never moved on to become the past, it would not be time but eternity. If, therefore, the present is time only by reason of the fact that it moves on to become the past, how can we say that even the present *is*, when the reason that it *is* is that it is *not to be*? In other words, we cannot rightly say that time *is*, except by reason of its impending state of *not being*. Yet we speak of a 'long time' and a 'short time', though only when we mean the past or the future. For example, we say that a hundred years is a long time ago or a long time ahead. A short time ago or a short time ahead we might put at ten days. But how can anything which does not exist be either long or short?"[47]

Taking his arguments still further, St. Augustine states that it is not correct to say that there are three divisions of time: the past, the present and the future. It would be more correct to say that there is the present of those things which have happened in the past, the present of present things, and the present of future things. These three exist in our minds: the present of past things in the memory, the present of present things in direct perception, and the present of future things in expectation. He concludes his argument as follows: "By all means, then, let us speak of three times, past, present, and future. Incorrect though it is, let us comply with usage. I shall not object or argue, nor shall I rebuke anyone who speaks in these terms, provided that he understands what he is saying and does not imagine that the future or the past exists now. Our use of words is generally inaccurate and seldom completely correct, but our meaning is recognized nonetheless."[48]

---

[46]*Confessions* 11,14, PL32,815.
[47]Ibid., 11,14-15, PL32,815-816.
[48]Ibid., 11,20, PL32,819.

Another fundamental difficulty is to be found in the actual measurement of time. St. Augustine points out that we measure time as it passes, because once it passes it no longer exists and therefore cannot be measured. At this point, he brings in the idea of space. "What are we actually measuring," he asks himself, "if not time, time in relation to some measurable space of time?" In truth, when we talk about periods of time and we say that they are 'as long as', 'twice as long', or 'three times as long', or if we start making any other division of time, all we are doing is measuring given expanses of time.[49] The writer thus comes to the conclusion that time is a space, the space of the mind, and the measurement of time is something that man does in his own mind where three functions coexist: those of expectation, attention, and remembrance. The object of his expectation passes out of his attention and becomes something that is remembered. The present is a fleeting moment, but what remains is the attention through which it passes on its way to becoming the past. The future is neither long nor short; what can be long or short is our expectation of it. Nor is the past either long or short, though our memory of it could be either.[50] So St. Augustine's conclusion is that the answer to the problem of time is not to be found outside the universe but within its confines, and he even goes so far as to state that it is not to be found in the external world of the senses but within the mind of man.

We also meet with similar views about time much later, in the works of Leibnitz (1646-1716). According to Leibnitz, time, like space, exists only in the imagination, and not in reality. He develops this in more detail, saying that: "Time, space, motion, and the continuum, as they are understood in mathematics, are purely imaginary things. That is to say that they are things which, like numbers, express possibilities." He then goes on to say that: "Space is the division of those things which can coexist, just as time is the division of those possibilities which obviously cannot coexist, yet exhibit a certain interdependence. Thus, the one concerns those things which exist with

---
[49]Ibid., 11,21, PL32,819.
[50]Ibid., 11,27, PL32,824.

each other at the same time or in the same place, while the other concerns all those things which, although they cannot coexist, one can think of them as existing, and thus, the one must follow the other."[51]

Newton (1642-1727) was a proponent of the idea of the real existence of both time and space. According to Newton, time and space have their own existence which is quite independent of the phenomena which occur within them. They are the instruments with which God activates his ubiquitous presence in the world while remaining present simultaneously in the past, the present and the future. This dualistic view of space and time has dominated physics even into our own time.

According to Kant (1724-1804), space and time constitute *a priori* categories that man employs when looking at the world, so that space and time are not empirical elements but imaginary moulds into which man places all those things that impose themselves on his senses.

It was Einstein, however, who ushered in a new epoch in speculation about time. Einstein's theory of relativity brushed aside the view that time has an intrinsic existence of its own, as it did the view that time is a fabrication of the intellect of man. The theory of relativity holds that there is no such thing as absolute time, but everyone has his own time, and this time depends on where he is and how he moves.[52] Time is thus directly connected with space and cannot be measured without reference to it. The combination of time and space creates a new dimension, 'time-space', where the various events which occur are to be placed. Finally, the past, the present and the future are all relative, since they depend on the kinetic state of the observer. We have thus abandoned the dualistic theory of space and time that dominated classical physics. It is worth pointing out that Einstein, who was the one who replaced the concepts of absolute time and absolute space with the concept of 'time-space', which cannot be understood in isolation from

---

[51] "Erwiderung auf die Betrachtungen über das System der prästabilierten Harmonie," in *Schriften zur Metaphysik* III,32.

[52] See S. Hawking, *A Brief History of Time*, New York 1988, p. 21.

the various events that constitute it, was of Jewish origin. It is not difficult to detect the presence of the biblical tradition in his theory.

We know today that time is polymorphic, as is the world with which it is linked and coexists. The conception of an earlier age, of time as something uniform, is belied not only by the personal experience of each and every one of us, and our resultant convictions, but also by the findings of modern science. Modern physics, in particular, teaches that in the various parts of the universe, there are different times, which are defined in accordance with the concentration or dispersal of matter to be found there. Time then, like space, does not only affect the things and forces of this world; it is also influenced by them. Just as we are unable to talk of events happening in the universe without reference to the concepts of space and time, so we are unable to talk of time and space outside the universe.[53] The various forms then, that time exhibits, are connected to the various forms and states of the cosmos.

---

[53]Cf. ibid., pp. 21-24.

Chapter Two

Time and Space

While time has been the object of intense study by modern thinkers, the subject of space* has remained on the sidelines, although in reality these two elements are inseparably linked. Time does not exist in a vacuum—it exists within space. Nor is space given to us of its own—it is given to us with time. Yet simultaneously, there does appear also to be a certain rivalry between time and space. Disengagement from a particular space or place requires a lapse of time, and movement within time always ends in a settling within space, which constitutes, as it were, the wastebasket of time.

This apparent opposition between time and space does not invalidate their unity. There are still analogies between them. Time as a measure of movement and change is not just a measure of growth and life, but also a measure of dissolution and destruction; while space, as the theatre of movement and change, is not simply an area of development and life, but also an area of decay and death. In fact, time as a measure of life offers man relative freedom within space. When his time is up, there is an end of his freedom too, as there is of his life within space. It is impossible for any form of freedom or hope to exist

---

*Translator's note: In Greek, the word *horos* is used in the sense of both 'space' and 'place,' and I have therefore used both in translating it.

in the world without the perspective of time.[1] The final subordination to space is a subordination to the sovereignty of decay and death.

Just as in the field of time a distinction is made between experiential time and abstract mathematical time measured by the clock, so in the field of space too, experiential space is distinguished from the abstract mathematical space which is calculated by objective measurements.[2] Finally, properties of space are attributed to time, just as those of time are attributed to space, so that we speak of long or short intervals of time, of infinite or finite space, and so on. Yet despite this, we can observe states or modes of life that are characterized, to a great extent, either by the sovereignty of space, or by the sovereignty of time.

Not only the ancient Greek, but the pre-Christian world outside the Bible is characterized largely by the predominance of space or place. Time here is not of prime importance, but is limited by, and recycled within, space. It is not in a position to transcend it. Even more than this, it has no real perspective. It is incapable of bringing about anything new. It is entrapped in the sphere where death holds sway.

The work of divine economy, on the other hand, creates a completely new perspective which sweeps aside the sovereignty of space and increases the importance of time, so that for Israel and for the Church there is considerable stress on the importance of time.[3] The call to Abraham to come forth from his land, from his kinsmen and from his father's house, is a call to an exodus from place.[4] Land, kin, and the father's house are categories of place. This exodus from *place* is only realized by

---

[1]"For the nature of time also, as it flows by, forms part of this perishable world... departing, as it does with those things that have perished, coexisting with those things that are happening, and being awaited and hoped for with those things that are yet to come." Basil, *Commentary on Isaiah* 66, PG30,232D.

[2]See O.F. Bollnow, *Mensch und Raum*, Stuttgart, Berlin, Köln, Mainz 1980 (4th ed.), pp.16-17.

[3]See M. Eliade, *Das Heilige und das Profane. Vom Wesen des Religiösen*, Frankfurt am Main 1985 (2nd ed.), pp. 97-98.

[4]See Gen. 12:1.

action within *time*. In this particular instance the exodus is accomplished as a result of the action instigated by God's promise, and man's hope that the divine promise will be fulfilled. Time tests faith and devotion to God.[5] Abraham puts his trust in God, forsakes things that link him with place, and hurls himself into a dynamic journey through time, in expectation of the fulfillment of God's promise.

God's promise to Abraham is associated with a new land.[6] It would be quite natural to ask whether this promise does not simply lead to yet another subjection to space. But this, however, is not precise. The new land to which Abraham is called has no intrinsic value of its own; its value is imparted to it by virtue of its being land designated by God—promised land. The abandonment of place is the *first* stage. The second stage to which man is summoned by God is that of abandonment of *self*. Thus the abandonment of place is supplemented by man's self-abandonment, or rather by the commending of the time of his life into the hands of God. This is what happens in the story of Abraham, and is repeated in the story of Moses.

Yet in the Old Testament, the place that is associated with a manifestation of God possesses a special importance. This place is sacred and is regarded with reverence and awe. Thus the place where Jacob in his dream saw the Lord and the ladder with the angels climbing up and down in the heavens, is called a 'fearful place,' the 'house of God,' and the 'gate of heaven.'[7]

In the same way, the site of the bush, where God appeared to Moses and called him to free Israel from the Egyptians, is called 'holy ground.'[8] The embodiment of all the holy sites of Israel is to be found in the temple. This, *par excellence*, is the place where God appears, where God dwells. It is in the temple that the man of faith draws near to God and finds authentic joy and contentment.[9] But the existence of the temple only has meaning as long as the people too remain faithful to their

---

[5] See Macarius of Egypt, *Spiritual Homilies* 9, 1-3, PG34, 532D-533C.
[6] See Gen. 12:1.
[7] Gen. 28:12-17.
[8] Exod. 3:5.
[9] See e.g. Ps. 26:4., 83:11-12.

Lord. When this does not happen, God permits the destruction of his temple in order to eradicate every false belief of his people.[10] This underlines the symbolic significance too of the temple as the place where God appears to his people. The fulfillment of this symbolic significance of the temple is stated by Christ when he issues his famous challenge to the Jews, with the words: "Destroy this temple, and in three days I will raise it up."[11]

Another feature associated with the abandonment of place is that of the long and arduous journey. The migrations of Abraham, like the exodus of the Israelites from Egypt and their journey to the promised land, are one continuous exodus from place and response to the call of God. But when the chosen people again are content with themselves in the promised land and forget their God, then it is granted to others to enslave and imprison them. The place, and especially the sacred place, is not offered to them for their repose and relaxation, but for remembrance of God's revelation of himself and preservation of the people's faithfulness before him. This is why it always has a symbolic and eschatological character.

For the Church, the promised land is the symbol of God's kingdom or the age to come. In other words, the place becomes a symbol of a new way of life or a new age that transcends the world's categories of space and time and refers us to the life of the world to come. The kingdom of God is not a particular place—it is eternal life; but eternal life is not a life without end within time, but the life in Christ. Christ is the land of the living, or the place of those who are saved. Space and time pass, "that God may be all in all."[12]

It is significant that this final transcendence of place, even of sacred place, is accomplished within the Church, where death is conquered. In other words, the victory over space, which is the sphere where death holds sway, is finally accomplished by the victory over death itself. This victory is in the

---

[10]See Jer. 7:3 ff.
[11]John 2:19. See also E. Jacob, *Théologie de l'Ancien Testament*, Neuchâtel 1955, p. 212.
[12]1 Cor.15:28.

process of preparation throughout the history of the Old Testament, which is the 'schoolmaster' leading us to Christ. The journey to the age of the Messiah is a journey of gradual disentanglement from space and dynamic movement within time. It is a journey that heads towards the *kairos* of the coming of the Messiah. The Church is not a *sanctuary* in the sense of being cut off or set apart from its surroundings, to be offered to God as a dwelling-place. The Church is the bridge that releases man from the tyranny of place and ushers him into the freedom offered by the Holy Spirit.

As with time, space too assumes a different character in the Church. It is transformed from an area under the tyranny of death into a place where God's love is revealed and man is transfigured. Furthermore, space does not confine the infinite, just as time does not diminish the eternal. The infinite is not just outside or beyond space; it is also to be found within it, in the same way that eternity does not exist solely outside or beyond time, but also within it. This is why every point in space too, by virtue of its being part of the content of infinity and therefore permeated by it, offers the possibility of incorporation into infinity. God is infinite, and the infinite God is everywhere in space without being confined or obstructed by it. The appearance of the infinite God in space as finite and circumscribed man constitutes the very foundation of the Church and the *sine qua non* for the renewal of the world and the deification of man.[13]

Confinement in space, even if it is sacred space, means a regression to Judaism. The Lord declared categorically that his coming signifies a release from all such confinement: "The time cometh when ye shall neither in this mountain nor yet at Jerusalem, worship the Father . . . God is a Spirit, and they that worship him must worship him in spirit and in truth."[14] This does not, of course, mean denial too of the pedagogical significance of sacred space which also has its place within the

---

[13]"The Word was indescribably wholly present here below, yet in no wise absent from the realm on high: God descended to earth, yet underwent no change of place." Kontakion of the Akathistos, Ikos Fifteen.

[14]John 4:21-24.

Church, where there is also a place for the whole of the Old Testament as a foreshadowing of the Body of Christ. But simply to reduce everything to this space, which is nothing but the abandonment of the body and a return to its shadow, is to ignore the truth. This is what those Jews who did not believe in Christ did, and another such deviation within Christianity is millennialism.*

It is characteristic that the expansion of the Church throughout the world is associated with the destruction of Jerusalem. Space, especially sacred space, when it is made absolute, is capable of restricting the power of the breath of the Spirit and obstructing and thwarting the freedom of the faithful. Besides, it must never be forgotten that worldly space is that sphere where death holds sway.

Space separates men. Even the various elements that bind men together in one particular region simply serve to separate them from the men of other regions. National elements, when they are set up as absolutes, turn themselves into idols. Thus national consciousness coincides with the worship of idols, and since national consciousness is always delineated by space, it becomes polytheistic. Those who have national consciousness cannot have monotheism. Monotheism presupposes a release from those elements of nationality which are tied up with a particular place. For this reason monotheism is, in principle, not possible in the static nature of place but only in the dynamic nature of time.

The prerequisites for the understanding of this phenomenon exist in everyday life. Men who live apart, separated by space, can live together, united by time. Many live simultaneously in a given moment of time, but are quite incapable of living simultaneously in a given point of space. Thus time unites those who are separated by place. But this quality of time is limited and relative, because eventually it wears them down and dissolves them. This unifying quality of time can only acquire its full value when it is joined to the victory over death.

---

*Millennialism, also known as millennarianism or chiliasm, is a teaching condemned in the early Church which is popular today among particular Protestant groups, stating basically that at the Second Coming, Christian believers will reign together with Christ on earth for a one thousand year period of peace and prosperity.

The Church brushes aside national consciousness and calls men to unity within time. All considerations of nationality, all those things, that is, that are associated with place, assume their proper proportions within the perspective of the eschatological expectation of the kingdom of God. The kingdom of God too takes on the multiplicity of mankind. The expectation of the kingdom of God unites the faithful in the one Church; and men *can* be united in the one Church, because it is in the Church that death is conquered and life is offered. Thus, in the Church men live in communion with the Triune God, as members of the Body of Christ by the grace of the Holy Spirit.

Any religion that fails to unite men within the perspective of the dynamic journey of time, is 'national,' that is to say idolatrous. It is subordinate to space, which is the region where death holds sway. But for this reason it is incapable of revealing the true meaning of history. This meaning is revealed only as a result of faith in Almighty God. With him, all the different versions of history are subsumed into the one history which makes its way towards the kingdom of God. For this reason, the revelation of God Almighty is the prerequisite for the revelation of the meaning of history. This revelation of the meaning of history is essentially the revelation of the end of history. At all events, history can only be interpreted in the light of the end of history. It has been accurately observed that "only the end of history can shed real light on its meaning, and it is only at the end of history that man will stand as master of history. This is why all interpreters of history have the tendency to imagine that they are living near to the end of history, regardless of the age in which they live."[15]

The possibility of such a view of history is provided in Christ. Christ offers man from the outset that which will be revealed at the *end*. If the journey of the history of man is compared with the journey to Emmaus, where at the breaking of bread Christ, who accompanied the disciples on their way, revealed himself, every breaking of bread is also, for those who participate in it, a revelation of the meaning of history.

---

[15] P. Tillich, *Der Widerstreit von Raum und Zeit*, p.131.

The Church, with her eschatological orientation, could be described as a community of exiles. The world sets up a place of temporary sojourn for it. The exodus of Israel from Egypt is a symbol of the Church's exodus from the world and its journey towards the heavenly Jerusalem, the kingdom of God. This is the true home of the Christian, while his earthly home is only the place where he resides or is given hospitality for a while: "every native land is foreign."[16] When the faithful sit back again in their own land and forget the kingdom of God, they lose their bearings. Yet at the same time, any place, insofar as it is the context in which the love of God can manifest itself, is familiar and dear to them: "any foreign land is home to them."[17] By offering themselves to Christ they are making an undertaking to resist sin and death within space. Monks are 'guardians of place.' They choose to confine themselves within space and there cultivate the spiritual freedom that Christ has offered them. They attach themselves to the domain of *death* so that they may live more intensely the expectation of the *new life*. They reconcile themselves to place, feel it as part of their own bodies, and transform it into 'Church' and direct it towards the kingdom of God.

---

[16]*The Epistle to Diognetus* 5,5.
[17]Ibid.

Chapter Three

Time and Life

Our lives unfold within time, and are determined by it; but how do we deal with time? How do we experience it in our everyday lives?

Time is usually divided into three parts: the past, the present and the future. But these three facets of time do not, in the final analysis, have any real substance. The present cannot be thought of as a duration of time, because if it were to be, then it too would have to be split up into past, present and future. The present can only be an infinitesimal or indivisible moment of time separating the past from the future. And this moment, although it is the only moment at our disposal, and therefore the only one with any real existence, becomes in point of fact inconceivable and nonexistent, for it immediately gives way to the past.

And yet, while the present is simply an imperceptible and fleeting moment, neither the past nor the future are available to us either, for the past is forever lost to us, and the future does not yet exist. Nevertheless, man does constantly have the sense of 'present'. He possesses this sense because he does not live time as a series of isolated moments, but as a more comprehensive reality, embracing both past and future. His memory and his hopes allow him to go beyond each specific moment and live the present as both synthesis and transcendence of past and future. Thus, the present in human life is presented as transcendence of time and leads to metaphysical ideas. It is interesting that ancient Greek mythology raised time to the status of a god, the god Chronos, who destroyed his own children.

St. Basil points out that time is our companion in life and leads us to the grave. Just as the ship's passengers are conveyed automatically to the harbor, even if they are asleep and therefore not aware of it, so each human being too, with the passage of time, as though in one continuous and relentless movement, is led to his end. "You sleep, and time races on ahead. You are awake, and you have various concerns, but life is being used up, even if it escapes your notice. We are all of us running down one road or another, each of us speeding towards his end . . . Everything passes us by and is left behind . . . Such is life. Neither its joys are forever nor its sorrows abiding. And the road is not your road, nor are present things yours."[1]

Man usually forgets the relentlessness of time, or at any rate dissociates it from his life and looks at it objectively. He sees it as something quite removed from him and therefore not directly concerned with his own life. He talks about the transitory nature of human existence, but understands this chiefly in relation to others. He knows that "all is in flux," but commonly holds himself exempt from this maxim. The thought that his environment will change and that many things will simply cease to exist presents no difficulty to him, but it is only rarely that he considers how the current of time sweeps everything away and will eventually destroy him too. He admits that everything is transient, but he considers it a virtual certainty that he himself will contrive to live to see their destruction and their passing.

This objectivization of time is a basic error, which alienates man and generates confusion and delusion. This deception was lent support and, in a way, 'institutionalized' by the wresting of man away from the natural and flexible time of the senses and the establishing of the objective and rigid time of the mechanical clock. But time is not a simple objective fact; it is a most profound existential process. It has less to do with physical phenomena and objects, than with human existence and life itself. This, moreover, is why the basic concept of the momentum of time, which is obvious and self-evident to the

---

[1] *Homily on Psalm* 1,4, PG29,220D-221A.

life and existence of man, cannot be incorporated into the laws of physics. Thus, to have the events of life take place in reverse order, as one might see in the cinema if a film were to be played backwards, is an incomprehensible, or even comic notion. The laws of physics, on the other hand, are symmetrical with regard to the course of time, and do not distinguish direction towards the future from direction towards the past, so that the eclipses of the sun in 4500 A.D. can be calculated with the same precision as the eclipses of the year 500 B.C.[2]

Men "are *polychronic* creatures. However much they are involved with the linear time of the course of natural phenomena, they nevertheless live lives that are adjusted to the rhythms of various individual times which are built deeply into the structures of the whole spectrum of the real world."[3] To every moment of the linear and irreversible time of natural phenomena, there corresponds a multitude of moments situated in various successive layers. Each of these layers represents a separate reality with its own content and its own particular structure.

Thus, corresponding to the seconds on the clock, there are, first of all, the seconds of an internal clock, which moves in cycles and regulates the movements and functions of the bodily organs. As has been proved by instances of people who have remained isolated from the outside world in underground chambers, this biological clock has a cycle of approximately twenty-five hours. What we have here is a 'circadian'[4] clock governing the human organism. In other words, the freely evolving biological cycle of sleeping and waking of a man who is isolated from the outside world lasts one hour more than it

---

[2] See G. Kontopoulos and D. Kotsakis, *Cosmologia. I domi kai i exelixi tou sympantos*, Athens 1982, pp. 245-246. For more on the subject of the course of time, see S. Hawking, op. cit., pp. 143-153 and P. Coveney-Highfield, *The Arrow of Time*, New York 1991.

[3] G. Mourevlou, *Metamorphoseis tou chronou*, p. 20.

[4] The term 'circadian', which was first used recently in America, derives from a synthesis of the two Latin words *circa* (about, approximately) and *dies* (day), and means 'approximately a day'. In nature there are many biological clocks. For more on these clocks see A. Winfree, *Biologische Uhren. Zeitstrukturen des Lebendigen*, Heidelberg 1986, and P. Coveney–R. Highfield, op. cit.

takes for the earth to revolve on its axis.[5] But this internal clock speeds up its movement in daily life, and adjusts to the rhythm of the external clock which is determined by the twenty-four hours it takes for the earth to revolve.

Apart from this clock, which regulates the cycle of sleeping and waking, there is another fundamental clock in the human organism, which controls body temperature. Associated with these two basic clocks, which determine a whole series of further clocks operating at various levels, are those special times which govern the various functions or states of the human organism. There is sleeping time, which is different from waking time, which is different in turn from cardiac time or respiratory time. Furthermore, internal time and the various specialist times move to one rhythm in childhood, another in adolescence, another in middle age, and yet another in old age. Finally, our experience of time in daylight is different from our experience of it during the hours of darkness, and again in the heat of summer it is different from the cold of winter.

The variety in the experience of time becomes greater when we move into the world of the mind. Feelings of joy or sorrow, longing or anguish, hope or despair, success or failure, create the sort of transformations in our view and experience of time which turn the meaning of the movement of the hands of the clock into some useful but purely conventional detail. What does one minute of time mean for each of those varied and contradictory states of mind that man may experience? What does a minute of joy or sorrow, a minute of hope or despair, a minute of pleasure or anguish at the approachment of death mean?

Finally, special categories are represented by the time of dreams and ecstasy. It is accepted that in the twinkling of an eye we can dream a multitude of things. The time elapsing between a loud noise and a sudden awakening can be sufficient to include a memorable dream.

But even more surprising is the capacity of time during states of spiritual ecstasy. It has been pointed out that "now

---

[5] J. Aschoff, "Die innere Uhr des Menschen," in *Die Zeit*, ed. A. Deisl, A. Mohler, München, Wien, 1983, p. 137. A. Winfree, op. cit., p. 20 ff.

and again the soul of the ascetic engaged in pure prayer touches upon genuine eternal life, her ultimate and unique aim."[6] In such states, the mind of man is "aware of everything simultaneously."[7] By the same token, the experience of hell too is presented as a time of never-ending torment.[8]

But macrochronically too, psychic time exhibits a quite separate peculiarity. In the human psyche, the past, of itself, does not exist. All that exists is the remembrance of it. The same applies to the future. All that exists is the expectation of it. Finally, the present does not exist as an indivisible and integral moment, but as a wider and deeper synthesis. It exists as *locus* of the time of our life.[9] This is why St. Augustine, instead of past, present and future, preferred to speak of the present of past things, the present of present things and the present of future things.[10]

A man looking back on his past sees his whole life condensed into the frame of one composite picture. Events that took place one or five or fifty years previously are gathered within the framework of an imaginary yesterday. Recent events disappear, while others of long ago appear in the field of vision. In the depths of the world of the mind, a reordering and reshaping of events is taking place, "which does not have much to do with chronology . . . Events, as memory presents them to us, often give us the impression that they have been transmuted, that the present acts formatively upon them and imparts to them a new meaning, or a meaning that it was previously impossible to imagine that they had."[11]

The secret dimensions of the world of the mind are hidden from us, but not done away with by the ordinary time of everyday life. However significant daily events may be, however

---

[6] Archimandrite Sophrony, *Saint Silouan the Athonite*, Essex, England 1991, p. 205.

[7] Op. cit., p. 49.

[8] Cf. Monk Paisius of Mount Athos, *O geron Hadjigiorgis o Athonitis*, Thessaloniki 1986, pp. 29-32.

[9] Cf. Archimandrite Eusebius Vittis, "O chronos ki ego. Prosopikes skepseis yia mia anthropini theorisi tou chronou" *Koinonia* 18 (1975), p. 230.

[10] See *Confessions* 11,20, PL32,819.

[11] G. Mourelos, op. cit., pp. 22-23.

fine the impressions are that external time makes on us, they are incapable of destroying the peculiarity of psychic time. How can positive developments in the world of politics, for instance, console a parent who sees his child destroying himself? What pleasure can a sunny day offer to someone suffering from toothache? When man attempts to dispel his unpleasant states of mind by being transported to some pleasant rhythm of external time, his success is relative and fleeting. He escapes to some extent from his pain or his sadness, but this too only lasts a little while. His psychic time, which had never really disappeared, soon re-emerges. When, again, he clings to social time and tries to bring everything into line with the conventional rhythm of the life of society, when he identifies himself with the spirit, the demands and the interests of those around him, he begins to act inhumanely, he sucks his life hopelessly dry, he becomes pathological, one-dimensional, 'monochronic'.

Modern man knows better than the man of any other age that things in this world are relative. Especially with the advent of inter-continental and space travel, he acquires clear experience of the relativity that exists, for example, between stillness and movement, between up and down, between night and day. We may stand motionless in a certain place, yet move with the earth at breakneck speed. We walk upon the earth and look at the sun in the sky, but even when night falls and we are in the opposite position, we still say that we are on the earth, although the sun is again in the sky but in the opposite position. What is day to us is night to the people of other lands, and what is winter for the people of one hemisphere is summer for the people of the other hemisphere, and so on.

But even those things which man considers to be the greatest opposites in his life, are in reality so relative that they lose their acuteness in an overall view. Thus, even the opposition between life and death finally disappears with the acceptance of the transcendental life that lies beyond the distinction between life and death. Life and death, which seem to be so different from each other, according to St. Gregory the Theologian, "in one way or another, come round to each other, and the one succeeds the other."[12]

Life, even as a biological phenomenon, constitutes an exception to the rule of the flux of time. As is known, time increases the entropy* of the world, and leads to disorder and disruption, ending eventually in so-called 'thermal death.'** The exception to this rule is the phenomenon of life. Life, while it moves with the momentum of time, overcomes the determinism of time, and reverses the course of entropy with the creation of order and organization amid the disorder and disruption. This phenomenon, however hard we may try to explain it away as 'self-organization' or a spontaneous emergence of order, making its appearance in the course of the journey of the universe towards thermal death, does not cease to represent a remarkable exception. In the final analysis of course, all living organisms are subject to the power of time and submit to death. Life is presented as the preliminary proceedings to death. But death too appears as the culmination of life.

Death as a biological phenomenon constitutes the final phase of life. This is more true of death as an existential phenomenon. But if death is the final phase of life, then life too acquires its full meaning with the summation of death in it. The need for the summation of death as existential phenomenon in life, and particularly for the experience of the presence of man in the world as a being that is destined to die, was emphasized in our century by the German philosopher Heidegger in his famous book, *Being and Time*.[13]

Since death then constitutes an essential feature of human life, man only finds the universal meaning of his life when he manages to include death in it as well. Here lies the impor-

---

*"The degradation of the matter and energy in the universe to an ultimate state of inert uniformity" or "the steady degradation or disorganization of a closed system" (quoted from *Webster's Ninth New Collegiate Dictionary*).

**A theory of the ultimate end of the universe according to the second law of thermal dynamics.

---

[12]*Oration* 18, 42, PG35, 1041A.
[13]M. Heidegger, *Sein und Zeit*, Tübingen 1967.

tance of the remembrance of death, which stands out in Christian literature as the means to spiritual perfection and joy. The remembrance of death eradicates the passions.[14] Divine compunction creates one unending festival.[15] This paradox derives from the nature of the spiritual life, which is radically different from mere biological life.

If biological life unfolds as the antithesis of the ravages of time, to which, nevertheless, it eventually submits, the spiritual life develops as the acceptance of the decay brought on by time, but only by harnessing it and placing it within the perspective of perfection and the aspiration to achieve the likeness of God. Man is both changeable and mortal. But he becomes immortal when he lives as a member of the Body of Christ, who conquered death. In this way, his capacity for change is transformed into capacity for the perpetual process of becoming more perfect and more godlike. The experience of this incessant drive for perfection and *theosis* is acquired by man in this present life already, in direct proportion to the purity of his heart.

Another fundamental illusion associated with the way we experience time is this: we are frequently oblivious to the meaning of our life in the present, and look for it in the ever-awaited future. Dissatisfied with what we receive in the present, we make a point of entertaining hopes for the future. "For the whole of man's life is like this," says St. Basil, "that not being satisfied with the here and now, he feeds not so much off what he has, but off what is to come."[16] Thus we busy ourselves, and make our way in the world as though we were going to live forever. And we usually complete our earthly life while still at the stage of preparing for the future.

Pascal, in his *Pensées*, says this: "We never remain in the present . . . We are so foolish that we allow ourselves to be swept away into a time that is not ours, without giving a thought to the only time that does belong to us. And we are so

---

[14]John Climacus, *The Ladder of Divine Ascent* 7, PG88, 796B. Theodore the Studite, *Epistle* 2, 134, PG99, 1429B.
[15]John Climacus, *The Ladder of Divine Ascent* 7, PG88, 808D.
[16]*Epistle* 42,1,PG32,349A.

conceited that we dream of those things which no longer exist, while at the same time racing without a thought past the only thing which does exist (i.e. the present). And we do this because the present usually wounds us. We close our eyes to it because it grieves us. And if it is pleasant we are sorry to see it go. We try to shore it up with thoughts of the future, and think of making available things over which we have no control, for a time that we have no certainty that we will actually see. If each of us were to examine his thoughts, he would see that they are ruled by the past and the future. We hardly give a thought to the present. And if we do think of it at all, we do so only to gain an insight into how to confront the future. The present is never our goal. The past and the present are means to an end, but our only goal is the future. Consequently, we never live, but always hope to live. And though we concern ourselves constantly with our happiness, it follows that we will never be happy."[17]

So it is that the future becomes a form of tyranny, while the present is simply the means of achieving future goals and aspirations. All of life's objectives are placed in the future, while the present is seen merely as a bridge leading to the future. And since what we actually live is not the future but the present, what actually happens is that we are constantly moving on the bridge, but without ever arriving at our goal.

This phenomenon took on a new form and development as a result of rapid advances in science and technology. The changes that were seen from ancient times up to the age of the industrial revolution in man's furthering of his capabilities, were not great, either in number or importance. The time, for instance, that would have been required to make a long journey in Homer's day, was much the same as would have been necessary in the time of Christ, or at the time of the Greek Revolution of 1821. On the other hand, however, the time required for any long journey on earth has been reduced to almost nothing in the last few decades. But in more general terms, too, the changes which in the past have taken place over whole centuries, happen now within a single day. At the

---

[17]*Pensées* 172.

beginning of the 1970s it was calculated that the sum of human knowledge would double within ten years. Today the doubling of human knowledge comes about even sooner; and because man is incapable of keeping abreast with the dizzy pace of change, and adapting to it, he quite literally loses himself, without actually realizing it.

Acceleration in the pace of change results in the acceleration of time itself. The remorseless succession of changes seduces man and refers him constantly to the future, since there is always the prospect of greater development yet to come. But with this sort of outlook, the man who dies can never reach the summit of the mountain because the summit is constantly shifting into the future. People of earlier ages could arrive contentedly at the end of their lives because there was no great puzzle left for them to solve. The great mystery for them was death itself, and this is why the phenomenon of death held such a central place in their lives, and why the study of death was the subject of such solicitude.[18]

But from the perspective offered by the notion of continuous development, death ceases to have any meaning, because it only serves to hinder man from keeping pace with the course of progress. And life too, in reality loses its meaning because it is seen simply as unending development without any real content or goal. Death, as the unavoidable end of life, destroys any meaning life may have held previously. It renders it nonsensical and absurd. But life too, or at least life as relentless progress which never achieves completion, is incapable of making any sense out of death. Thus, the price that man pays for his insatiable appetite for uninterrupted progress and affluence, and the fruit that he bears for his unconditional surrender to the conquests of science and technology, are his general disorientation and alienation, not only from his environment, but also from his very self.

And yet, a radical change has already taken place. Science and technology, which have made comfort and prosperity possible, have robbed man (and especially the young, who were born and have been brought up with them) of patience and

---

[18] M. Weber, *Le savant et le politique*, Paris 1959, pp. 79-80.

discipline. Distances have been reduced to nothing, and huge obstacles have been overcome. Incredible distances are covered in a short time and without trouble, while insuperable difficulties are swept aside easily and effortlessly. Man has become detached from space; an entirely new relationship has been established between space and man. Space, just like time, now stands revealed as a sphere, the destruction and dissolution of which man is actually experiencing. His familiarity with space has been undermined. He sees it as a sphere where he wrestles with all his powers, even though he is certain of his ultimate defeat. He thus remains unreconciled with space. He travels everywhere, but finds rest nowhere. He readily changes locality, because everywhere he goes he feels a stranger and rootless. He is forever searching for a new place, but the one he takes up is not really any different from any of the previous ones.

Space is indissolubly linked with time. But while space presents itself as neutral, allowing movement in any direction, time presents itself as rigid, sweeping everything along in the same irreversible direction. And even the slightest reversion in this relentless flow of time appears impossible. Time does not turn back. Despite all this, however, man seeks a release from time, and finds his outlet in the future. He receives further encouragement in this from the possibilities available to him today for forecasting and, to some extent, determining the future. Thus, whatever gives him pleasure in his dealings with space, he looks for in his dealings with time too. Just as he is able, tirelessly and impatiently, to traverse huge distances and arrive at the ends of the earth, so he wishes, tirelessly and impatiently, to traverse huge spans of time and arrive at the very end of history. The same way of experiencing space is sought after in his way of experiencing time. And the same facilities that have been extended to the one sphere are pursued in the other too. The genre of science fiction, with its tales of men traveling in machines that traverse time, is particularly expressive of this phenomenon.

Man today does not want to submit to the ordeal of time before he arrives at his particular goal; he wants that goal attained immediately. He does not possess the patience needed to wait in expectation; he is governed by the 'convenience' mentality. Just as he sees that every far-distant point in space can quickly and easily be made to be 'here', so he thinks that any distant point in time, and especially in the future, can quickly and easily be made to be 'now'. He has no aversion to what is far off. On the contrary, he likes it and wants it at his feet. Equally, he is not averse to what is in the future. This too he likes, and wants now, as 'present'.

Modern man is the man of the 'here and now'. He does not see any final goal in his life to which he can also subordinate the various smaller goals that motivate his actions. And the lack of any final goal actually reduces to nothing all the various smaller goals, while at the same time investing these very goals with a form of finality. He uses the vehicles of science and technology to the utmost in his life; yet he perceives that he is at once unable to satisfy his spiritual needs with them, or to avoid the contradictions inherent in his material aspirations.

Nikita Khrushchev, during a reception for representatives of the African republic of Mali in Moscow in 1962, said that radical political movements offer to change things here and now, to create a paradise on this planet, in opposition to Christianity which promises a paradise after death.

The things of the spirit and of eternity are usually ignored or thought of as utopian. Despite this, however, man does not completely lose his spiritual yearning, or abandon his eschatological view of time. Even the most fervently secular man of our day never ceases to desire something higher and more permanent. He does not cease to hang on at least to the shell of the eschatological view of time, which the Christian tradition shaped over the centuries. In the final analysis, he does not deny the *eschaton* that religion professes—it is just that this too he wants here and now. He wants it both 'of this world' and easily accessible. So in one sense we can say that modern man is eschatological. But he wants the *eschaton* to be perceptible within the present. He does not want to wait for it, he does not want to hope for it, nor does he want to prepare himself for it, or to put himself out on its account. Seduced by the possibilities of science and technology and by his own impatience, he demolishes the future in order to create a capacious present for himself.

The possibilities afforded to mankind by modern science and technology, but also the needs man has created for himself by his new mode and rhythm of life, have allowed him to employ and make use of, or even foresee, the future in the present. All the great scientific, technological, economic, political and other programs of our age are, in effect, advance plans for, and anticipations of, the future. So it is that the future is no longer open and free for the man who will live then, but is to some degree already assumed for him in the present, mapped out for him and already paid for by default. At the same time, the freedom of the man of the future is restricted and mortgaged to the schemes and programs of the present. In an earlier age, children used to receive a dowry from their parents. However, today's parents are depriving their children of their natural dowry. This deprivation is in danger of proving fatal to the survival of those children.

This situation, which is all too apparent in all walks of society, is brought home in fairly dramatic fashion by the current ecological crisis. The exhaustive use of sources of energy, the pollution of the environment, and the disturbance of the ecological balance—all serve to make use of, predict and anticipate in the present the possibilities and prospects of the future. None of us as individuals remains outside this polymorphic complex of programs and specifications for the future, which are continually being drawn up in the present. Moreover, the same mentality also affects to a great degree the personal lives of the men of our age, except that in our age, the incidence of the unexpected and the uncertainty of the programs and drafts for the future, remain more intense.

This phenomenon has created the new theory of time and especially the new understanding of present and future. In this context there is talk of a rediscovery of time in our day,[19] or of prolongation of the present at the expense of the future.[20] At

---

[19]See M. Elchardus, "The Rediscovery of Chronos: The New Role of Time in Sociological Theory," *International Sociology*, vol. 3 (1988), p.35 ff.

[20]See H. Nowotny, *Eigenzeit. Entstehung und Strukturierung eines Zeit-*

the same time, however, new responsibilities are created too, which impose new forms of behavior on man. Today, more than at any other time, human behavior cannot take account of the static nature of place alone, but must also take account of the dynamic nature of time too. This acquires ever greater importance in human life, and for this reason must be evaluated seriously when it comes to organizing it and serving it.[21]

Over and above any changes there might be on a social level, the time of life of the faithful still has its unique value and its special orientation. Time becomes *kairos* of communion with God. This communion, which has a personal and mystical character, remains invisible to the world. St. John Chrysostom, addressing the 'newly illumined' members of the Church, and explaining the direction that their life takes on after baptism, says this: "Your life now remains hidden and undeclared to those who do not believe. But there will come a *kairos* when it will become manifest. Now is not your *kairos*."[22]

The Christian, once he joins the Church, refers his life and the time his life affords him, to Christ. Without ceasing to be in the world and live the life of time, he is transposed "to another city."[23] He puts his time, or as St. Chrysostom says, his *kairos*, on another plane of life. Thus, the life of the man of faith unfolds on two levels: the temporal and the eternal. On the first level, time is seen as man's enemy and provokes his reaction to it. He wants to 'kill' time, or to 'have a good' time, that is, to dissipate and dissolve the boredom to which it gives rise in his heart. The sort of phrases we use in everyday life are revealing. On the second level, life is seen as man's friend and aid. It is treated as a gift offered by God as the means of man's renewal and perfection of himself. The more a man ages physically as he stretches towards the future, the more he

---

gefühls, Frankfurt am Main 1989 (2nd ed.), p. 47 ff.

[21]See G. Mantzaridis, *Isagogi sti Ithiki. I Ithiki stin krisi tou parontos kai tin proklisi tou mellontos*, Thessaloniki 1990 (2nd ed.), p. 67.

[22]*Catechesis* 7,22, ed. A. Wenger, Jean Chrysostome, *Huit catéchèses baptismales*, in *Sources Chrétiennes*, vol. 50, Paris 1957, p. 240.

[23]Op.cit., 7,23, p. 241.

renews himself spiritually and becomes "a newer version of himself."[24]

Since man's life in time is influenced by sin, his span of life too has to be a time of repentance and avoidance of sin, and in this connection, the relevant petitions and exhortations that are often repeated in divine worship are characteristic: "That we may complete the remaining time of our life in peace and repentance, let us ask of the Lord."[25] Peace, which is first and foremost inner peace from passions and sin, but also peace in our personal relationships and in society—like repentance, which is the one and only means of restoring and making something positive out of the negative aspects of our past—is the most fundamental precondition for our going forward in life creatively. The next and final goal in life for the man of faith is a Christian end, and his good defense before God.[26]

A man's whole lifetime, however many years it lasts, is extremely short when compared to eternity. But the correct use of time during this present life brings eternal profit. An image that is often used in order to portray the nature of this present life is that of the festival or fair. St. Gregory the Theologian's remark is typical: "Think of this life as a fair, at which, if you trade well, you will show a profit."[27] The believer is called to exploit the time afforded to him in this life, by trading what is ephemeral for what is eternal.[28] He is called to spend the whole time of his life observing the commandments of God and putting up with every grief and difficulty, in order to gain eternal blessings.[29] There can be no better investment of his time.

---

[24]See Basil, *Homily on Psalm 32*, 2, PG29, 328B.

[25]Litany in Orthodox divine services.

[26]"That the end of our lives may be Christian, without torment, blameless and peaceful, and that we may have a good defence before the fearful Judgement–Seat of Christ, let us entreat the Lord." Ibid.

[27]*Theological Poems* 33, PG37,930.

[28]"Let us do a deal with time. Let us trade that which cannot last for that which abideth." Gregory the Theologian, *Oration* 17,11,PG35,977.

[29]See Ephesians 5:16, and Symeon the New Theologian's commentary thereon, *Ethical Discourses* 12, ed. J. Darrouzès, Syméon le Nouveau Théologien, *Traités théologiques et éthiques*, in *Sources Chrétiennes*, vol. 129, Paris 1967, p. 384 ff.

All things in the world are bought at a price corresponding to their value. And yet the eternal life which Christ promises is bought at a very small price. Even if a man dedicates every single year of his life wholly to God, he cannot possibly tip the scales in his favor. Not only that, but while man's contribution is of this world, his reward is of heaven. Thus, this temporal life is offered to the man of faith as *kairos*, that is, as an opportunity for good trading and eternal enrichment.[30] By avoiding the wickedness of the world and growing rich in the fruits of the Spirit, he becomes a shareholder in eternal life.

---

[30]"This time we are given in this present life of ours is a *kairos* for trading for every man." Symeon the New Theologian, *Ethical Discourses* 12, 91-92, op. cit., p. 390. Cf. also the second sticheron of the aposticha in the First Tone, for Friday evening: "You have achieved sanctity by your good bargaining! For you have shed blood, and inherited heaven; you have undergone trials and now exult forever. Your trading has been good indeed."

Chapter Four

Christ and Time

When the timeless God comes into the world, he makes an unprecedented incision into time and history, and lays the foundations of a new and qualitatively different age. The whole of human history before Christ was a period of preparation for the coming of Christ. This preparation was made within the milieu of the chosen people of God, but also on a wider scale, throughout mankind. St. Paul the Apostle, in his letter to the Galatians, writes: "But when the fullness of time was come, God sent forth his Son, made of woman, made under the law, to redeem them that were under the law, that we might receive the adoption of sons."[1]

But the question arises: How is the phrase, 'the fullness of time,' to be understood here?

As we have already seen, in the Old Testament, there is no concept of an absolute time, which is given so that events can be recorded. Time without events is not comprehensible. And the chief events are God's manifestations of himself to the world. It is these that give time its meaning and its content. It is these that determine its nature and its rhythm.

Time, then, cannot be understood in its own right. And we should not look for the 'fullness of time' in its inaccessible and indeterminate nature. The fullness of time is to be found in the fullness of the events which are played out within time. It is to be found in the completion of a process of dialogue and struggle between God and man, which prepared the way for the appearance of God as man in the world.

---

[1] Gal. 4:4-5.

God, by his active presence in the history of Israel, and his steadfast faithfulness to his promises, constantly asked his people for faith in, and compliance with, his will. And as the fulfillment of these preconditions approached, the coming of Christ was being prepared and foreshadowed. Isaac, Joseph, Moses, Joshua and the Prophets all prefigured, and prepared the way for, the coming of Christ. But the fullness of time was reached when that woman appeared who was to be able to give birth to Christ: the Virgin Mary. The whole process of preparation reached its culmination in her person, and it was in her that eternal salvation had its beginnings.[2]

Christ, who is the Son of God and the bearer of God's kingdom into the world, comes as the last "emissary of God."[3] His Incarnation constitutes the end of the age of the law and slavery, and heralds the beginning of the age of grace and adoption. The whole work of creation is summed up in the work of regeneration in Christ. The Word of God, who was present "in the beginning," assumes and renews those things which the book of Genesis tells us were created "in the beginning."[4] In this way the purpose of the existence of man and of the whole of creation is reinstated.

Christ is the new, but also the last, Adam.[5] He is the reason for, and the purpose of, the world. He is he who exists before all else, and in whom all is sustained: "For by him were all things created, that are in heaven and that are in earth, visible and invisible . . . all things were created by him, and for him."[6] So in Christ, time too has its beginning and its end.

---

[2] "She it is who is both cause of those who preceded her, and protectress of those who succeeded her, and responsible for bringing us to eternity. She it is whom the prophets foretold, who is the first of the apostles, the support for the martyrs, and the firm foundation of the teachers." Gregory Palamas, *Homily 53*, 25, in *Gregory Palamas, Archbishop of Thessaloniki: Twenty-two Homilies*, ed. S. Oikonomou, Athens 1861, p. 162.

[3] Mk. 12:6. Cf. Heb. 1:1-2.

[4] See Jn. 1:1 ff. Cf. also O. Cullmann, *Christ and Time*, Philadelphia 1977, p. 131.

[5] See e.g. 1 Cor. 15:45-49.

[6] Col. 1:16.

Christ and Time

The coming of Christ disrupts the course of the world. The events that he brought about "once and for all"[7] in history, create a new world, while at the same time establishing a new time that is radically different from the time of everyday life, as it is from the sacred time of mythology. And yet it is something of a challenge to the secular man, and even to the religious man, to accept that during the brief period of Christ's presence, and especially during the final days of his life on earth, the salvation and renewal of the universe were accomplished.[8] It seems to be a foolish proclamation that eternal life was offered to man through the Passion, Death and Resurrection of Christ, which happened under Pontius Pilate.

But at the same time, this new time which was established with the coming of Christ brings a content and a perspective to the time of everyday life that mythical time attempted, but was unable, to offer. The yearning of man for victory over death and participation in eternal life, which mythology tried to cover by referring it to mythical time, is satisfied now in history by the 'once and for all' self-offering of Christ. Thus, the mythical preface which runs 'Once upon a time . . . ,' and refers us to a fictitious time[9] that is constantly recycling itself, is now confronted by the prelude to the Gospel readings, 'at that time . . . ,' which refers to the specific and unique time of the presence of Christ in history.

Christ renews the whole of the universe. But as God–man, or *theanthropos*, he has a special relationship with man. He sums up the whole human race, and leads it to its final destiny. Time, which was created together with the cosmos, and rules man and his life, becomes woven into eternity. The visible is united with the invisible, and the created with the uncreated. Man becomes god and is freed from the constraints and limitations of his nature. His position in the world is transformed and his relationship with time is redefined.

---

[7] See Heb. 7:27, 9:22, 10:10.
[8] See Gregory Palamas, *Homily* 51, PG151,521CD.
[9] For more on mythical time see M. Eliade, *Das Heilige und das Profane. Vom Wesen des Religiösen*, Frankfurt am Main 1985 (2nd ed), p. 63 ff.

Christ is not only the new and last Adam, who has come in order to regenerate the old; he is also the model of the old Adam. Man was created for Christ from the very beginning. "For it was for the new man that human nature was established even from the very beginning," says St. Nicholas Cabasilas. And he goes on: "It was towards Christ that man's mind and desire were oriented. We were given a mind (*nous*), that we might know Christ; desire, that we might run to him; memory, that we might remember him, because even at the time of our creation, it was he who was the archetype. The old Adam was not the model of the new, it was the new Adam who was model of the old."[10] Whatever the descendant of the old Adam wants of his life, wherever he turns amid the temporal limitations of his earthly existence, whether it is towards the future in expectation, or towards the past in remembrance, it is only in Christ that he can find his fulfillment.

Yet this recognition of the new Adam as model of the old already ignores the direction of time and inverts the natural temporal sequence. First becomes last, and the last becomes the archetype of the first. This complete reversal is not the result of an arbitrary whim, but the consequence of the union of the divine with the human, the eternal with the temporal. Christ, the new Adam, is the archetype of the old, because the old Adam was created in his "image and likeness." At the same time, however, Christ is the pre-eternal and timeless God who, within the confines of time, assumes the mortal and finite nature of man in his own hypostasis.

The hypostatic union in time between the timeless God and human nature renews nature and time. Created nature is not ignored, but rather created anew and illuminated by the uncreated grace of God. Time too is not disdained, but renewed and pressed into the service of the incorruptible and the eternal. It is in this way that Christ brings about the new state of being, the new creation.[11]

Christ did not come into the world with a mere semblance of human form; he came as a real human being, "made of a

---

[10]*On the Life in Christ* 6, PG150,680A.
[11]See 1 Cor. 5:17.

woman."[12] The Son of God, who is perfect God, became perfect man too. Furthermore, the Son of God did not appear 'as though through a channel' from the Panagia,* but took from her his created human nature. The Panagia, according to one of the hymns of our Church, is "she who inexpressibly bore within time him who is without time."[13] She is that woman by means of whom "both nature and time are formed anew."[14] With her flesh and her blood she gave human form to God and gave birth to him as a man within the world. By means of the perfect offering of her life within time to the God who is without time, she became the *Theotokos*, the Birth-Giver of God, and "the cause of the deification of all men."[15]

But Christ too came into the world in order to offer as man his life and his lifetime to God for the salvation of the world. The crowning moment of Christ's life was the moment of his Death.[16] Christ lived the hour of his impending Death in the utmost sadness. He besought his Father to deliver him from it, but at the same time realized that his mission was to arrive at that hour: "Now is my soul troubled, and what shall I say? 'Father, save me from this hour?' But for this cause came I unto this hour."[17] Thus, the life of Christ reached its fulfillment in death. And the end of his life marked the accomplishment of his mission: "It is finished."[18]

In biblical and patristic tradition, particular emphasis is placed on the tangible presence and appearance of Christ in heaven, on earth, in hell, in the waters, and in the air. There is no place and no time that has not been visited by the divine energy or light of Christ. Christ, as St. Paul the Apostle says, is

---

Panagia ("All-Holy"): a name often used by Orthodox Christians when referring to the Mother of God.

---

[12] Gal. 4:4.
[13] Megalynarion for the feast of the Ascension.
[14] Dismissal Hymn for July 2, Commemoration of the Placing of the Honorable Robe of the Most Holy Theotokos.
[15] Akathist Hymn, Troparion of the Sixth Ode.
[16] See Jn. 7:30, 8:20, 13:1, 17:1.
[17] Jn. 12:27.
[18] Jn. 19:30.

"he that descended . . . into the lower parts of the earth" and he "that ascended up far above all heavens, that he might fill all things."[19] The Cross of Christ is life and resurrection for mankind,[20] while his Burial is the gate of paradise for the human race.[21] Finally, the Resurrection of Christ regenerates the world and fills all things with light.[22]

Christ, says St. Nicholas Cabasilas, does not disdain time, for he himself appeared within time. Moreover, just as he illuminated earth and hell by staying for a certain length of time in each, in the same way he stayed for a little while in the air during his Ascension, in order to sanctify it too. Indeed, quoting the relevant passage from St. Luke, "He was parted from them, and carried up into heaven,"[23] Cabasilas notes that Christ ascended into heaven "slowly and gradually," and not in an instant, so as to sanctify the air which contained him, even for a little while.[24]

The work of the salvation and renewal of the world is accomplished by the Father, through the Son, in the Holy Spirit. With the Incarnation of God in Christ, human nature has been renewed and the foundations of the new creation have been laid. And it is this fact that constitutes the aim of divine economy. It is the event that embraces the whole of creation and gives history its meaning, sweeping aside all constrictions and limitations of time. Christ himself says: "Your father Abraham rejoiced to see my day: and he saw it, and was

---

[19]Eph. 4:9-10.

[20]"Thy Cross, O Lord, is life and resurrection to thy people." Sticheron at Lauds (the Praises) for Sunday in the 2nd plagal tone.

[21]"The deified soul went down into hell, so that, just as the Sun of Righteousness has dawned for those on earth, so too the light may shine for those dwelling in the darkness and shadow of death under the earth; so that just as he preached the gospel of peace to those on earth . . . so too he might do so for those in hell." John of Damascus, *Exposition of the Orthodox Faith* 3,29, PG94,1101A.

[22]"Now are all things filled with light, the heavens and the earth and the regions below the earth." Troparion of the Third Ode, Paschal Canon.

[23]Lk. 24:51.

[24]*2nd Sermon on the Ascension of the Lord*, Nicholas Cabasilas, *Epta anekdotei logoi*, ed. B. Pseftongas, Thessaloniki 1976, pp. 114-115.

Christ and Time

glad."[25] The vision of the day of the Lord that was given to Abraham and to the prophets of the Old Testament, was given to them by the power of the Holy Spirit. But for the saints of the Church too, it is only in the Holy Spirit that the glory of the Lord is visible. The Spirit of God, unfettered by any limitation of time or place, initiates man into a personal communion with God, and offers the faithful the renewal that is in Christ.

The setting in which this renewal in Christ is maintained and offered, is the very Body of Christ himself, the Church. In the Church, by the grace of the Holy Spirit, the world, and with it, time, receive regeneration. 'Now' becomes the receptacle of eternity, is transformed into 'forever' and exists always: 'to the ages of ages.' In this way a new view of time and the concepts associated with time, takes shape.

God, as creator of the ages, is not simply eternal, but pre-eternal or everlasting. The ideas of the eternal and eternity, which were associated with ancient philosophical or theological understandings,[26] relate to and are connected with, the created world of the spirit. On the other hand, ideas about that which is always the same, the everlasting, are not connected with the created world but refer to the uncreated God.[27] That which is eternal is not necessarily everlasting as well, although this was a presupposition in the thought of Plato. The eternal is that which is immortal. The soul of man, as being immortal, could be called eternal. But this immortality is radically different from Plato's immortality because it is not self-existent, but created. Self-existent immortality, according to Christian teaching, is possessed only by God, who is uncreated. It is he "who only hath immortality."[28] And this divine immortality

---

[25] Jn. 8:56.

[26] See e.g. Plotinus, *Enneads* 3,7,5: "Wherefore the eternal is holy, and our thoughts tell us the same in respect of God."

[27] "But there are already some who demand that the ages too should be called everlasting, on the grounds that since they are always present they have acquired this appellation. We, on the other hand, account it sheer madness to say that creation bears witness to the everlasting, while depriving the Lord of creation of the same admission." Basil, *Against Eunomios* 2,17,PG29,608CD.

[28] 1 Tim. 6:16.

does not concur with the eternal and eternity, but with the 'everlasting'. However, there are times when the terms 'eternal' and 'eternity' are used to mean the same thing as the 'everlasting'.[29] At all events, in contrast to God, who is by his nature eternal and everlasting, man is by his nature a temporal being.

Man's temporality is a function of his created and mutable nature. The deification which is offered in Christ, and represents the final goal of man's existence, does not revoke his created nature and his mutability, but transforms them. By sharing in the uncreated grace of God, man is freed from the corruptibility of the world and partakes of eternal life. Thus man, who is created in time, becomes eternal and without end by virtue of having taken part in the eternal and unending life of God. He receives by grace everything that God has, without becoming the same as the divine essence. His advancement has no limit. The end of this journey of his represents a fresh beginning, and the beginning contains all the fullness of the end.[30]

Yet in the teaching of the Fathers, we also find an even more surprising position. The man who shares in the grace of God and becomes a god by grace, is rendered not only eternal and without end, but also unoriginate and everlasting.[31] This is

---

[29]As John of Damascus points out, the word *aeon* can mean: "a man's lifetime, or again . . . a period of a thousand years, or again . . . the whole of this present life, and the age to come—that which is without end, and comes after the resurrection, or again . . . neither time itself nor a part of time . . . but that which is coextensive with everlasting things, like some temporal period and interval. For as time is to those under time, so *aeon* is to those things which are everlasting . . . There is then only one creator of all the ages, and that is God, who has created the universe, and exists before all ages." *Exposition of the Orthodox Faith* 8,1 (15),PG94,861B-864C.

[30]"In the end they will have the beginning, and in the beginning the end." Symeon the New Theologian, *Hymn* 1,190, ed. J. Koder, *Sources Chrétiennes*, Vol. 156, Paris 1969, p.172.

[31]"He became without either beginning or end, no longer bearing within himself that life which is subject to time and change, which has beginning and end, and is beset with much suffering, but rather the divine life alone, of the indwelling Word, which is everlasting and not brought to an end by any death." Maximos the Confessor, *De Ambiguis*, PG91,1144C.

not, of course, attributable to his own created nature, but rather to the uncreated grace of God. The created and temporal nature of the man of faith is confined to the context of his earthly existence. When this ceases, the life without beginning and without end, that is of Christ, that exists and acts within him, manifests itself.[32]

This position is simply a natural consequence of the Church's teaching on the deification of man. Just as red-hot iron, without ceasing to be iron, simultaneously becomes fire as well, so too the deified man, without ceasing to be man, simultaneously becomes god. Without ceasing to be a creation of God, he becomes a partaker in the divine life and attains the eternity that is of God. He becomes not only eternal, but also unoriginate and everlasting in the image of the eternal and unoriginate and everlasting God. He becomes a son of God, because the Son of God too became man and united himself with man.

Christ is the light of the world.[33] Man's participation in the Body of Christ—the Church, is participation in the light of Christ. And the looked-for manifestation of the kingdom of God is, in fact, the manifestation of the divine light that is to illumine the faithful. This is why the eschatological experience of the kingdom of God too is an experience of his uncreated light.

The idea of light dominates Orthodox theology, and perceptible light is the most expressive symbol of the presence of God. We know today that matter is energy, and energy is matter. Thus, the whole of creation is reduced to energy, and this energy represents the created work of the uncreated divine energy. With the coming of Christ then, and the accomplishing of his regenerative work, the whole of creation receives the

---

[32]"Paul, then, was 'created' only as long as he was living the life which was created *ex nihilo* by the command of God. When he was not living this life, but the life that has reached the indwelling of God, he became 'uncreated' by grace, just like Melchisedech and all those who have acquired the Word of God alone living and working within themselves." Gregory Palamas, *To Akindynos* 3,16, in *Syggrammata*, ed. P. Chrestou, Vol. 1, Thessaloniki 1962, p. 308.

[33]John 8:12.

regenerative energy of God, so that it can be transformed into new creation.

At this point we should perhaps comment on something that the Lord himself says when referring to the last day: "But of that day and that hour knoweth no man, no, not the angels which are in heaven, neither the Son."[34] For the Son, who is consubstantial with the Father, this seems a strange thing to say. How is it that the Son does not know the last day? The Fathers of the Church usually say that he does not know it as man. But this does not mean that he does not know it as God either. And for him to know it as God, without knowing it as man, must mean that this day is not accessible to man. So, in other words, this knowledge can be considered unattainable within the category of time into which Christ entered by virtue of his Incarnation.

Something similar could be said about the two occasions where Christ says: "The hour cometh, and now is."[35] These two things cannot both be true at the same time. The hour that has not come, but is on the way, cannot also exist as "now." And the hour that exists as "now" cannot be on the way, because it is already here. This saying can only be true if we transcend the limitations of time.

Yet today we also meet with ideas that are to some extent similar in the field of physics. The relativity of time and the absence of synchronicity are sufficient proof of this. Thus, for example, an objective appointing of a particular "day and hour" for the end of the universe would be quite conventional. But what meaning does the assigning of a particular moment of the earth's time, or indeed the appointing of the time of its destruction, hold for the universe? Or what meaning does the moment of destruction of a distant galaxy in the universe hold for the earth?

The end of the world can be compared with its beginning. Just as the beginning of the world cannot be placed in a particular moment in time because it is precisely with this that time begins, so the end of the world too cannot be placed in a

---

[34]Mark 13:32.
[35]See John 4:23, 5:25.

particular moment in time, because it is precisely this which marks the end of time. The end of the world means the end of time. And just as the end of the world means its elevation to the kingdom of God, so too the end of time entails its reduction to that reality which transcends time, that "now" of the presence of God,[36] in which its beginning too is to be found.

Also connected with the end of the world is the "day of the Lord." In the Old Testament, and especially in the prophetic books, this term is used with a wide range of meanings, and indicates the intervention of God in history, or his final appearance in order to restore righteousness.[37] In the New Testament, the "day of the Lord," which is also called the "day of Christ,"[38] is closely linked to the Second Coming of Christ, but without actually being identified with it or losing its wider meaning.

Christ, as we have said, notes that Abraham desired to see his day, and "he saw it and was glad."[39] The "day of the Lord," therefore, or of Christ, has already arrived with his coming into the world. But at the same time, this day is awaited as the day of the Second Coming. It is that day on which the heavens will disappear and the elements of nature will burn and dissolve. The faithful wait according to God's promise, for "new heavens and a new earth... wherein dwelleth righteousness."[40]

On the basis of what has already been said, it becomes clear that the "day of the Lord" cannot be confined to the last day or the Day of Judgement. To give such an interpretation would be to ignore both the meaning the phrase has in most books of the Old Testament, and Christ's own affirmation that Abraham saw this day and rejoiced in it. The "day of the Lord," as the day of the manifestation of his glory, has a very broad meaning.

---

[36] See Basil, *Commentary on Isaiah* 119, PG31,312A.
[37] See e.g. Amos 5:18-20. Joel 1:15, 2:1, 3:14. Zech. 14:1. Isa. 13:6. Ezek. 13:5, 30:3. For more on this, see G. von Rad, *Theologie des Alten Testaments*, Vol 2, p.129 ff. and D. Kaimakis, *I imera Kyriou stous Profites tis Palaias Diathikis*, Thessaloniki 1991.
[38] Phil. 1:10, 2:16. Cf. also 1 Cor. 5:5. 2 Cor. 1:14. Phil. 1:6.
[39] John 8:56.
[40] 2 Peter 3:10-13.

The fullest rendering of the meaning of the "day of the Lord" is given, we think, by St. Symeon the New Theologian. According to him, the "day of the Lord" is called this not because it is "the last of days," or the day of the Second Coming, or the Day of Judgement, but because it is then that God will shine with the glory of his divinity.[41] It is then that all perceptible things will give way, and there will be "only he alone, God and his day together."[42] For those who become "sons of light," and "sons of day," and behave as sons of light and day in their lives,[43] the "day of the Lord" is already come. These people are already living the "day of the Lord" and contemplating his glory. These things, of course, do not come about simply as a result of a formal receiving of Baptism and the Holy Eucharist, but rather through real communion and union with Christ. And just as Christ is not limited by time and space, so the experience too of his presence, or the experience of his "day," is not confined to the 'eschata,' the last times, but is offered here and now.[44] The *eschata* will not present entirely new things, but will manifest in their full and perfect form, those things which exist and are offered already as a sort of betrothal in the Church.

---

[41]"So it is called the day of the Lord not because it is the last of these present days, nor because he must come on this day, in the same way that we speak about these days of the present time . . . but neither is it called Day of Judgement because judgement is to take place on this day (for it is not the case that the Day of Judgement is one day, and that the day on which the Lord is to come is another day), but because he, the God and Master of all things, will shine at this particular time in the glory of his own divinity." Symeon the New Theologian, *Ethical Discourses*, 10, 11-20, ed. J. Darrouzès, Sources Chrétiennes, Vol. 129, Paris 1967, p. 260.

[42]Op. cit. 10,26, p.260.

[43]See 1 Thess. 5:5. Rom. 13:13. Eph. 5:8.

[44]"Those men, therefore, that become children of that light, and sons of the day that is to come, and are able to walk honestly, as in the day, to these men, the day of the Lord will never come; for they already live in it always and forever. For it will not be to those who constantly shine with the divine light, but to those who are in the darkness of their passions and living in the world and desiring the things of the world, that the day of the Lord is suddenly to be revealed, and will be considered dreadful by them and like unto a fire that cannot be put out." Symeon the New Theologian, *Ethical Discourses* 10, 132-140, op. cit., p. 268.

Chapter Five

Church and Time

The coming of Christ brought the kingdom of God into the world, and the place where the kingdom of God is made manifest is the Church. It is the Church that introduces eternity into history and offers history the perspective of eternity. The Church is the Body of Christ, which transcends place and time and joins mankind to a communion that is beyond time, a transcendent communion where all things are present in the Holy Spirit. In the Church, time and the whole cosmos are redeemed. Whatever God has offered to the world is to be found in the Church and passed on to man for his salvation and regeneration.

The kingdom of God is not simply awaited as something that is to come; it is also perceptible as something now present. The resurrection and regeneration in Christ as well are not only awaited in the future, but are also already offered in the present: "The hour is coming, and now is, when the dead shall hear the voice of the Son of God: and they that hear shall live."[1] The voice of Christ, which has already been heard, and has summoned men from death to life, will also summon those who are in the tombs and grant them life. The hour which is coming, but which is also already present, is the hour of the presence of Christ. It is Christ himself. The *eschata*, the last things, exist in the last Adam, Christ. The things hoped for are already offered in his person. The period of the presence of Christ and his Church is the period of the "last days."[2] It is the

---
[1] John 5:25.
[2] See Acts 2:17. 2 Tim. 3:1. Heb. 1:2. James 5:3. 1 John 2:18. Athanasios,

period during which God and his kingdom are made manifest in history.[3] It is the beginning of eternal life, which cannot be interrupted by death.[4]

The Transfiguration and Resurrection of Christ are already manifestations of the kingdom of God in the world. And the times after the coming of Christ are the last times. The manifestation of the glory of God in the Church with the descent of the Holy Spirit on the day of Pentecost, like the personal manifestations we encounter in the saints of the Church, are eschatological events. And the experiences of these events are experiences of the last manifestation of God, which, since they take place in space and time, where corruption and death continue to exist, are of the "knowing in part"[5] kind. Thus, the *eschata* are at once present yet awaited, experienced yet expected.

The founding of the Church brought about the communion of God with man. The uncreated and eternal God was united ontologically with created and mortal man. Eternal life manifested itself in temporal life. Created and mortal man thus becomes through grace uncreated, eternal and everlasting, or, in other words, unoriginate, because the grace which regenerates his existence is uncreated, eternal and unoriginate. There is nothing left anymore to prevent the joining of created and uncreated, temporal and eternal, present life and life to come. The time of the realization of these events is 'last' time. The day and the hour are 'last.' Nothing else is awaited, neither Messiah, nor Paraclete, nor Antichrist. All things are present—Christ, and the Paraclete, and the Antichrist. Christ is present with the Holy Spirit in the Church, and the Antichrist is present too as an evil spirit that makes war on the Church.[6]

Against the Arians 1,55, PG26,125C.
[3] See Matt. 16:28. Mark 9:1. Luke 9:27.
[4] See S. Agourides, "Chronos kai aioniotis (eschatologia kai mystikopatheia), en ti theologiki didaskalia Ioannou tou Theologou," *Epistimoniki Epetiris Theologikis Scholis*, vol. 3, Thessaloniki 1958, p. 156.
[5] 1 Cor. 13:9.
[6] "Little children, it is the last hour and as ye have heard that Antichrist shall come, even now are there many antichrists; whereby we know that it is the last hour." 1 John 2:18. Cf. ibid. 4:3. For more on the Antichrist, see my

Church and Time

The presence of the Antichrist constitutes an eschatological phenomenon not so much in itself, as in relation to, or, to be precise, in contrast with, the eschatological presence of Christ. All those things which the incarnate manifestation of God in history have a share in bringing about (i.e., his Crucifixion and his Resurrection) create the last times, the last day, the last hour, which exists here and now.

The *eschata*, then, the last things, are not limited to the end of history, but exist already in the life of the Church. The last times encompass the whole period following the coming of Christ. And Christ who is "the Alpha and Omega . . . which is, and which was, and which is to come,"[7] is the Lord, the beginning and the end of history. Whoever has Christ, has life.[8] The experience of this life already exists in the Church. The renewal and deification of man in Christ, which is awaited in the age to come, is already lived in this life: "Now are we the sons of God, and it doth not yet appear what we shall be: but we know that, when he shall appear, we shall be like him; for we shall see him as he is."[9]

Although it is revealed to the world "through a glass, darkly,"[10] the kingdom of God does not cease to be truly present. The symbols whereby it is offered to us are neither metaphors nor analogies, but real symbols. The uncreated light of the Transfiguration, the Resurrection, Pentecost, and that which is seen by the saints of the Church, is the light of the kingdom of God. It is the real symbol of its presence.

The great mistake at this point, which is made chiefly by western theology, is to understand the symbolic or "in part" manifestation of the kingdom of God to the world as a metaphor or an analogy. This position was decisively refuted by St. Gregory Palamas during his dispute with Barlaam of Calabria. The light of the Transfiguration, which is the same as the light that the saints of the Church see, is not a created symbol of

---

study, *Orthodoxi theologia kai koinoniki zoi*, Thessaloniki 1989, pp. 126-135.
[7] Rev. 1:8.
[8] 1 John 5:11.
[9] 1 John 3:2.
[10] 1 Cor. 13:12.

the kingdom of God, but a natural symbol of it. In other words, it is the light of the kingdom of God itself, which manifests itself "in part," so that it becomes accessible to man. Just as the dawn, which issues from the light of the sun, is the natural symbol or portent of its appearance, so too the uncreated light which manifests itself in the Church, constitutes the natural symbol of the kingdom of God.[11]

The eschatological character of the Church is revealed more especially in the mystery of the Holy Eucharist. The celebration of this mystery is the central and eschatological act *par excellence* of the Church. It is her *Leitourgia*, that is, her very way of life. It is the Eucharist that constitutes the perfect communion which transcends the divisions of space and time and reveals the kingdom of God to the world. Participation in the Holy Eucharist means communion with Christ, sharing in his eternal life,[12] and entering into his kingdom. These things are not just presented metaphorically, they truly take place and are offered as real experiences to the members of the Church. Christian life has an experiential character, and the content of this experience is the presence of the kingdom of God. The life of the faithful within the Church presupposes this presence, is directed towards it, and is nurtured by it.

Participation in the kingdom of God brings about an eclipse of time, just as the presence too of the kingdom of God in the world does away with the divisions of time. The *Leitourgia* of the Church, that is, the Holy Eucharist, which is also the pledge of the kingdom of God, turns all understanding of the logical sequence of time on its head. It is the supper at which Christ offers his body and blood before his Crucifixion, and which continues to be offered after his Resurrection.

The Church of Christ is not just another scattered social group, but a universal society. And she is universal because she extends not only "everywhere in the universe," but also "every-

---

[11]See Gregory Palamas, *Defence of the Hesychasts* 3,1,14, in *Syggrammata*, vol. 1, Thessaloniki 1962, p. 628. *Answer to Akindynos* 5, 8, 33, in *Syggrammata*, vol. 3, Thessaloniki 1970, p. 311.

[12]See John 6:33-37.

Church and Time

where in time."[13] The Church still stands as a sign of eternity in the world and guides the world towards eternity. The institutions of the Church, as St. Basil points out, transport the mind of man "from things present to the things to come." And he goes on to say that it is thus that the man of faith, every time he prostrates himself and then stands upright, gives practical testimony to the fact "that through sin we have fallen to earth, and through the love of mankind of him who has created us, we have been called back to heaven."[14]

The simple yet eloquent example of the prostration gives St. Basil the opportunity to mention the new dimensions amid which the life of the Christian unfolds. Once he has accepted God's love of mankind as power which raises from earth to heaven, man perceives new orientations in the linear time of history. Eternity imbues temporality, so that every day, every hour, every second in linear time assumes unlimited breadth and fathomless depth, becoming a receptacle of eternity, and offered as the possibility of communion of the finite with the transcendent. It becomes possible to share in the eternal while living in time. And time is not confined to an elusive and irreversible flow, but every moment of it offers man the possibility of placing himself within the boundless love of the eternal God.

The Church is not subordinate to time, but leads from time into eternity. As the Body of Christ, and as communion of deification, the Church brings the world into the kingdom of God. But again as Body of Christ and communion of deification, the Church makes manifest within the world the kingdom of God. The world and the kingdom of God are linked and woven together, thus creating the eschatological period of the presence of the Church. The time of history becomes the 'locus' of our entrance into eternity.

Transcendence of the world is effected in Christ within the Church through the grace of the Holy Spirit.[15] The Church

---

[13] John Chrysostom, *Commentary on Psalms*, 144,4,PG55,469-470.
[14] *On the Holy Spirit* 27,66,PG32,192C.
[15] Cf. "Let grace draw near, and let this present world pass away." *Didache* 10,6.

does not dissolve along with the world. The end of the world, which will also be the end of time, will not also be the end of the Church. The Church leads to the kingdom of God. And just as the kingdom of God does not receive its revelation all at once, but rather by a gradual process, so the end of the world too does not come all at once, but is presented first as prelude and then as completion. The prelude to the end was the destruction of Jerusalem, and its completion will be the final destruction of the world.

In referring to the end of the world, Christ likens the destruction of Jerusalem to the destruction of the world, and ends with the following assurance: "Verily I say unto you, this generation shall not pass, till all these things be fulfilled. Heaven and earth shall pass away, but my words shall not pass away."[16] The destruction of Jerusalem came about before the passing of the generation to which Christ spoke. And the final destruction will come about before the passing of the generation of Christians.[17]

The end of the world, just like its beginning, cannot be placed in a particular moment of time. The beginning and the end of the world are understood by man only in relation to their conventional place in time. Thus, without actually constituting subjective phenomena, they are unavoidably associated with the subjective position of man in history and are impenetrable as part of the will of God. It would therefore be more correct if we were to talk not about the end of the world, but the *mystery* of the end of the world, which will also be the mystery of the end of time, just as we ought to speak of the mystery of the beginning of the world, which is also the mystery of the beginning of time.

Before time, and also after time, there is eternity and everlastingness which are beyond time.[18] Time acquires meaning

---

[16] Matt. 24:34-35.

[17] For the interpretation of the word 'generation' as generation of Christians, see John Chrysostom, *Homily on Matthew* 77, PG 58, 702.

[18] "There was a particular state that is older than the creation of the world and befitting to the supernatural powers, the state of being beyond time, eternal, everlasting." Basil, *Hexaemeron* 1,5, PG 29, 13A.

because it is associated with eternity and does not exist without it. It becomes real history, because it is united with eschatology.[19] History has no meaning without some end to it. And the end of history, after the coming of Christ, exists in every single moment of history. Thus, the Church's understanding of history is to be found in the unlimited depth of each moment of history, and not in the external successions in the flow of time. The length of time and history acquires value only when their depth is turned to account. And it is the depth of time and history which offers the only real justification of their length.

The limitation of time to one-dimensional movement leads unavoidably to disappointment and disenchantment. The history of civilization is a history of disappointments, and so-called Christian civilization, as a creation of man in linear historical time, shares the same fate. But what the Church offers is a way out of the secular impasse. She represents the transition from the aimless flow and eddy of time into the fullness of divine love and life.

Secular space and secular time are associated with the deception of the world. Nevertheless, they are turned into positive factors when they are used as occasions for entering into the truth of eternal life. This present life, observes St. Basil, is in fact death. The life to which Christ calls man is quite different.[20] It is the life that is not subject to the deception of the world and the disappointment of death. It is the life that transfigures man and places him beyond human capabilities and perspectives. It is the life of the kingdom of God, which manifests itself in the Church of Christ and is offered to man here and now.

The Christian is called to use his time properly and to invest it in the constant perspective of eternal life.[21] The relativities and irregularities of this present life are not so much

---

[19]See O. Clement, *Transfigurer le temps. Notes sur le temps à la lumière de la tradition orthodoxe*, Neuchâtel 1959, p. 130.
[20]*Homilies on Psalms* 33,9,PG29,373A.
[21]See Eph. 5:16. Col. 4:5.

negative states or insignificant episodes in our lives, as possibilities for moving away from "those things which are seen and move, to those things which stand still and do not move."[22] In this perspective, all things find their place and their justification. Nothing is abandoned. Nothing is overlooked. Nothing is looked on as mere coincidence. God is the Lord of the world and of history, the 'Overseer of all' and Ruler of all. Joy and grief, success and failure, progress and catastrophe do not cancel each other out, but are offered as means of the fulfillment of man, of the complete perfection of his life, which is realized in the Church.

The Church does not abhor time, but manifests herself in time. She does not grieve for time that has passed, nor is she anxious over that which is to come. The close of the day that passes becomes the beginning of the day that is to come. Every Vespers service leads us into the new day. And while a man may grieve over what he has lost, or be happy over what he is expecting, and while he may regret the past and be fearful of the future, the Church calls him steadily and resolutely to a journey which involves placing himself in the hands of God, of God who is the Lord of time and history—the *Pantocrator*.

This position of the Church puts an end to fragmentation and creates unity. The faithful reflect on the day that has passed and repent for whatever evil they have done and for whatever they have lost. This would have no meaning if it was a process which concerned lost time. What has happened cannot be altered, and whatever is lost cannot be won back. If, on the other hand, irrespective of what happens and what is lost, man can live and be redeemed; if, irrespective of the time that passes, the time at man's disposal continues to be *kairos*—the opportunity for redemption and resurrection, then the problem of time is solved.

This is what happens in the Church. Irrespective of what happens and what is lost each day, the day's end is the beginning of a new day. And each new day is a new *kairos*, a new opportunity for drawing near to the one and only "day," the

---

[22]Gregory the Theologian, *Oration* 7,19, PG35,780B.

Church and Time

"day of the Lord." It is a symbol of the day which is the Lord himself: "day and God together."[23]

By her manifestation in the world and her progress through history, the Church redeems and guides the faithful. She does not take away their past, she simply incorporates it creatively into the present. She does not allow them to lament over time that has been lost, but she does help them to reach forward to the future that is to come. She does not allow their tears to be lost in the past, but channels them so that they water the present and bring forth fruit in the future. She thus reaches out into history with her Body, which is the Body of Christ, "the fullness of him that filleth all in all."[24]

The Church of Christ moves within the world with her own time. This time, of which we will now speak at greater length, accompanies secular time and flows into eternity. Thus she holds man and the world in unity. She prevents disintegration, and guides man towards his fulfillment. Issuing from the wellspring of life and heading towards the fullness of life, she forms an endless stream of life for the whole world, keeping the mystery of the presence of Christ alive in the world.

---

[23]Symeon the New Theologian, *Ethical Discourses* 10,11 ff., Sources Chrétiennes, vol. 129, p. 260.
[24]Eph. 1:23.

Chapter Six

The 'Diachronic' Tradition

It is tradition that nurtures the diachronic* unity of men in history. Tradition presupposes corruption and death, yet at the same time fosters regeneration and life. Tradition is a kind of death which harbors life; and the acceptance of tradition means acceptance of death as agent of life. Life is preserved wherever it can be fostered by the decay and destruction which time causes. When life that is disappearing does not nourish life that is in the process of being brought forth, then the life that is coming into being remains in a state of suspension.

Tradition unites society that is prone to disintegration, and human society is characterized less by unity than by fragmentation. St. Nicholas Cabasilas invokes the very close relationship and communion that is created between parents and children, and observes that: "Children are unable to acquire their own hypostasis unless they are separated from their parents. The separation is that which from the outset makes the one parents and the other offspring."[1] True communion, he says, exists "when the same thing exists at the same time in both."[2]

---

*The word 'diachronic' is a transliteration from the original Greek meaning 'trans-temporal', or 'that which runs through time'.—*Trans.*

---

[1] *On the Life in Christ* 4, PG150,601B.

[2] "True communion consists in this: that the same thing is present simultaneously to both parties. When, however, both parties have it, the one at one time, the other at another time, it is not so much a sharing as a separation." *op.cit.*, PG150,600D (trans. by deCatanzaro, St. Vladimir's Seminary Press).

The 'Diachronic' Tradition

Time is offered as a unifying factor in social life. People who are contemporaries can have true communion. But time can also become a fragmenting factor in social life; for those who are not contemporaries cannot have true communion.

As well as time, which unites, but also divides men, there is also space. Space is offered essentially as agent of "separation" or division. People who live at the same *time*, cannot also live in the same *space*. Two people can be in the same space only at different times. The union in time imposes a separation in space. But space is also offered as an essential of human society, for separation and distinctiveness are *sine qua nons* for the manifestation of the character and composition of society. Yet these factors already restrict the fullness of society.

The facts of man's location in time, and separation in space, represent at once potentials for, and obstructions to, the development and preservation of human society. Tradition, as a factor which links men who are distanced from each other by both time and place, fosters society. Tradition is founded on memory, which preserves society's diachronic unity. Place gives shape to tradition. And when tradition that is shaped in place does not preserve its diachronic unity, it does not last as tradition.

Tradition means our paternal home, or, in a wider sense, that place which is ripe with the memories of our parents and forefathers. Our relationship with our 'place' is a relationship with our tradition. To guard our 'place' is to guard our tradition. And this is what Orthodox monks do—they 'guard the place.'

But every place where men live is linked to a particular way of life. And this way of life shapes the particular local tradition, which leaves its imprint, to a greater or lesser extent, in customs and symbols. Man either accepts his tradition, or distances himself and alienates himself from it. Acceptance requires a spirit of cooperation and unselfishness, for when individualism and selfishness prevail, tradition is scorned or simply exploited to the advantage of the individual. When a man accepts his tradition, he fosters it and breathes life into it, whereas when he rejects, or selfishly exploits it, he destroys it, and turns it into just another objective value. In the first case, tradition operates creatively and links diachronically those who identify with it. In the second, it is stifled and becomes incapable of acting as a bonding agent.

Tradition means movement and life, which is why it cannot be cultivated simply by hanging on to it, but only by organic development and renewal. And traditionality does not mean conservatism, but creativity. There is respect for the past, but also creative progress towards the future. Traditionality can be expressed as conservatism only temporarily, when objective factors prevent its functioning smoothly. When tradition becomes identified with 'hanging-on', it loses its identity and is stifled.

Christianity is offered as tradition, while at the same time it introduces a new dimension into tradition. In other words, what it does, in essence, is to create its own tradition, which is usually called sacred tradition. This tradition of Christianity has Christ at its core, and the preservation of the tradition consists in the world's entering the Body of Christ—the Church, and remaining there. Tradition is the way of the Church. This is what preserves the diachronic unity of the Church. But at the same time, it is also the *truth* of the Church. It is her defense against the oblivion of the corruptible world, which leads to destruction. Finally, tradition is the *life* of the Church. It is the liturgical and worshipful communion of her members with Christ, the source of life.

The tradition of the Church is summarized in the mystery of the Holy Eucharist: "For I have received of the Lord that which also I delivered unto you, that the Lord Jesus, the same night in which he was betrayed, took bread: and when he had given thanks he brake it, and said, 'Take, eat; this is my body which is broken for you: this do in remembrance of me.' After the same manner also he took the cup, when he had supped, saying, 'This cup is the new testament in my blood: this do ye, as often as ye drink it, in remembrance of me.'"[3] The Holy Eucharist is the mystery of the Church. It is the mystery of

---

[3] 1 Cor. 11:23-25.

The 'Diachronic' Tradition

Christ, in which the faithful share in the Holy Spirit. In the mystery of the Holy Eucharist, the Church offers the essence of her tradition, that is, Christ who is broken yet not disunited, eaten yet not consumed, is divided and yet unites.[4]

There are also, of course, many more specific traditions, written and unwritten, which the faithful are called to keep. Thus, St. Paul writes to the Christians of his day: "Brethren, stand fast, and hold the traditions which ye have been taught, whether by word, or our epistle."[5] And during post-Apostolic times many traditions were preserved and took shape in the life of the Church. But the center of all these traditions is, and continues to remain, Christ. Tradition without a direct or indirect link with Christ has no meaning in the Church, and the importance of the various traditions of the Church is in direct proportion to the extent of their relation to Christ.

All the traditions that are associated with Christ have a eucharistic or worshipful character. This is why they are offered "in a mystery." "Of the dogmas and preaching that have been preserved in the Church, some we have from written teaching, and others we have received handed down to us *in a mystery* from the tradition of the Apostles."[6] This tradition "in a mystery," is no apocryphal tradition. It is that tradition which comes about through the mysteries, or sacraments, especially Baptism, Chrismation and the Holy Eucharist.[7] The Church is founded on these mysteries and in them is summed up the complete theandric (divine–human) economy.[8] Participation in the mysteries of the Church means participation in the Church's tradition.

This sacramental tradition "in a mystery" is preserved in the world as the Church's tradition. And the Church exists as the sphere where the grace of the Holy Spirit is made manifest. The arrival of the grace of the Holy Spirit means the passing of

---

[4] Prayer at the division of the Holy Lamb before Communion, Liturgy of St. John Chrysostom.
[5] 2 Thess. 2:15.
[6] Basil, *On the Holy Spirit* 27,66, PG32, 188A.
[7] See G. Florovsky, *Bible, Church and Tradition*, Belmont, Mass. 1987, p.86.
[8] See John Chrysostom, *Homily on John* 85, 3, PG59, 463. Gregory Palamas, *Homily* 60,3, ed. S. Economou, p. 250.

the corruptible world, and the grace of the Holy Spirit comes in accordance with the extent of the passing of the corruptible world. The Church cannot exist as locus of the manifestation of the Holy Spirit unless, within it, decay is overcome and the world is transfigured. When the Church is confined to what is tangible and immediate, she becomes part of the world and estranged from grace.

In the *Didache of the Twelve Apostles*, we find the prayer: "Let grace draw near, and let this present world pass away."[9] During the first centuries of her existence, the Church combined this prayer with her life as "a society in exodus." In this way, she lived constantly the transcendence of the world and the presence of grace. The gathering strength of the institutional dimension of the Church, and the secularization of the faithful, which were felt after the recognition of Christianity as an official state religion, stifled the charismatic dimension of her life.

It was then that the Church's tradition was renewed in monasticism. The emergence of monasticism created new potential for the transcendence of the world and the manifestation of grace. Thus the living Body of the Church, which spread to ever wider areas of the world, won in the desert a new and vital place for the manifestation of grace. And always, where the Church remains alive, she acts as an integral body, replacing the decay which her presence in space and time entails.

The Church cannot preserve her identity in history without developing organically in time and space. And the Church's preaching cannot be offered unaltered to the world without adapting in an appropriate way to her respective environment. Adaptation of the way in which tradition is offered in accordance with the needs of the environment constitutes a prerequisite for the preservation of its content. If the method of presentation remains unchanged, then either the Church's tradition is distorted or her conventional presentation to the world is in vain.[10]

---

[9] *Didache* 10,6.
[10] G. Mantzaridis, *Christianiki ithiki*, Thessaloniki 1991 (3rd ed.), p. 283.

The 'Diachronic' Tradition

Orthodoxy is traditional. Its traditionality expresses not the singularity of Orthodoxy, but its catholicity. But the catholicity of Orthodoxy also constitutes at the same time its singularity. It is its chief characteristic. The Orthodox tradition is not just another confessional tradition, but the tradition of the undivided Church. And here lies its singular importance for the whole world. There do, of course, often appear Orthodox churches and Orthodox theologians who treat tradition as closed and impenetrable. This can represent a confessional tradition, or even an 'orthodox' confessional tradition, but not Orthodox tradition as it has been experienced and cultivated in the undivided Church.

Tradition as progress and life sometimes takes the form of innovation. There are many such instances in the history of the Church. Thus, the use in the Creed of the term *homoousios* (consubstantial) was considered by many theologians in the fourth century to be an unacceptable modernism. Yet this word conveyed in the best possible way the unalterable content of the Church's tradition. St. Symeon the New Theologian, who used his experience of the life in Christ to oppose the conventional religiosity of his day, was also considered a modernist by many of his contemporaries. Finally, St. Gregory Palamas, who gave the reply of Orthodox tradition to the challenge of his time, was labeled a 'new theologian' by his opponents, and his teaching described as 'the new theology.'[11]

Orthodox tradition is not to be identified with any particular 'establishment,' but with Orthodox faith and life. And the observance of the tradition of Orthodoxy does not mean simply preserving what has been objectivized by the Church, but rather becoming part of the life and spirit of the Church, this life and spirit always having their foundation in the Holy Eucharist—the sacrament of the communion of God with man. It is this that initiates the diachronic unity of the faithful and introduces eternity into time.

---

[11]See Gregory Palamas, *Answer to Akindynos* 6,16,61 and 5,26,105 in *Syggrammata*, ed. P. Chrestou, vol. 3, Thessaloniki 1970, pp. 432 and 368. Cf. also Akindynos, *Iambics against Palamas*, PG152,849B.

Western Christianity as a whole rejects tradition deep down. Of course, we cannot fail to distinguish 'traditional' Roman Catholicism from 'anti-traditional' Protestantism, but this distinction does not run very deep. Roman Catholicism neglected tradition as a source of unity based on memory, curbing its interest in the past, and seeing tradition more as unity in the present. It shifted the emphasis from that of unity based on memory to that of unity based on an institution, and squeezed tradition into the confines of conformity to type. The tradition of the Fathers was swept aside, and adherence to tradition came to mean agreement with the Pope and his representatives. In this way, however, tradition lost its roots and its durability in time. It was undermined as agent of diachronic unity and became limited to the role of simple geographical link. It lost its potential for promoting organic development and led to the quandary: conservatism or innovation?

Love of tradition in Roman Catholicism came to be identified, as was natural, with conservatism. This was, to begin with, the characteristic feature of Roman Catholicism. But conservatism proves itself to be inadequate, especially in the modern pluralistic reality. Conservatism can do nothing in the face of the ravages of time and comes into conflict with life itself. The Church becomes fixated in the past, and her mission of renewal is held back in the present. The dead have no place in the fellowship of the present, while the living are trapped in the fellowship of the past. Thus, with the sanctioning of the sovereignty of the past, the importance of both present and future is stifled. Love and hope, as virtues of the present and the future, are made subordinate to a dead *credo* which, eschewing its eschatological orientation, is transformed into mere ideology.

On the other hand, innovation abhors the decay associated with time, and is incapable of accepting it in the present as an agent of life. The faithful become cut off from the past and stay suspended in the present. The dead are absent from the fellowship of the present, while the living are reduced to improvising for a fellowship in the future. Thus, a pattern of the unending reform of things is established and anything of any duration is considered wearisome. Faith loses its historical verification, while hope and love are, in essence, reduced to individual emotions. This phenomenon emerged originally in Protestantism, in which, as we know, the view was held that the Church needs to be constantly reforming herself: *Ecclesia semper reformanda*. If the Church is not being reformed, then she cannot preserve her identity. But Protestantism, which denies historical tradition, leads not to organic development, but to actual alteration of the Church. The example of Protestantism and the pressures exerted by the needs of contemporary society have already exercised a profound influence on Roman Catholicism too.

The question of the correct consideration of tradition is, in the final analysis, a question of the correct consideration of time and space. And since we usually either do not want, or do not have the courage, to delve into the heart of the question, we confine ourselves to a superficial understanding of it. However, in so doing, we create a fictitious relationship with space and time which either leads us to a superficial approach to problems, or makes us out of step and utopian.

The question of the consideration of space and time is a question of whether, and to what extent, man refers the questions to a transcendent reality. Without this reference, any understanding of space and time is fragmentary and limited. But even this reference, within the data of space and time that define man and his life, is in fact, impossible or imaginary. The only real possibility of reference to a transcendent reality is offered in Christ. It is in the person of Christ that the temporal is united with the eternal, the finite with the transcendental. Union with Christ within space and time is union that transcends space and time. It is a union which brings about the relation to a transcendent reality and true communion.

This union with Christ comes about in the Church by the grace of the Holy Spirit. The Church is the Body of Christ. And the tradition of the Church is the life of this integral and undivided Body with its diachronic unity and its union beyond time with Christ. The tradition of the Apostles, the Fathers and the saints of the Church, which preserves the diachronic unity of the faithful in history, initiates us into the mystery of the communion with Christ that is beyond time. And the preservation of this communion with Christ beyond time is the basis for the diachronic safekeeping of the tradition of the Church. Christ, who recapitulates the past, the present and the future,[12] keeps perpetual and indissoluble communion with all the members of his Body, the Church. The tradition of the Apostles, the Fathers and the saints of the Church ministers to this communion between God and man, and finds in it its summary and final expression.

The tradition of the Church is not a simple objective commodity to be possessed by successive generations of the faithful. A tradition such as this might perhaps have great value, but it could not also guide the life of the Church. And it cannot guide the life of the Church because it is impossible for it to lead to true communion: "When the same thing is not at the same time with both parties, but now the one has it and now the other, there is no communion, but rather separation, for that which unites does not exist, since it is not with both at the same time."[13]

Tradition is received by incorporation into the Body of the living Christ, and preserved as life and way of life within the sphere of decay and death. Tradition as communion with Christ does not offer only the *eschaton*, but also the sign which leads to the *eschaton*. It is not just the treasury of the kingdom of God, but also the symbol of this treasury. This, moreover, is why it cannot function correctly in the Church without its eschatological vision. When the Church's tradition is cut off from its eschatological vision, it becomes an idol or an ideology and is incapable of fulfilling its purpose. This is where the tremendous danger in conservatism lies, when it is transformed into an established order within the Church.

Orthodoxy has a painful history. All the Orthodox Churches were in the past, or are still in the present, in difficult external circumstances. These often obliged them to take refuge in conservatism, so that they could preserve their iden-

---
[12]See Rev. 1:8.
[13]Nicholas Cabasilas, *On the Life in Christ* 4, PG150,600D.

tity. This phenomenon had detrimental consequences for the Churches' dealings with the problems of the day. Conservatism, in the sense of devotion to the past, constitutes a considerable danger for the Church when it is changed into an established order. If the danger is to be overcome and the living tradition—which is in a position to deal creatively with the problems of the times—is to be preserved, resolute faith and intense effort are required.

Chapter Seven

Monasticism and the Church: Biological Discontinuity and Spiritual Continuity

Biological discontinuity is the characteristic feature of a special section of the Church, the monastics. In monasteries, men and women are not born, they only die. Life in the monastery is a preparation for death; and yet the preparation for death, like death itself, is here full of life.

The institutionalization of biological discontinuity in monasticism culminates in the breaking off of every biological relationship, in order to attain a universal spiritual relationship and diachronic continuity. Monastics do not have children. They have no natural successors. In fact, they do not have parents either, for they give up their parents when they are tonsured, with that 'passionless hatred' that Christ himself taught.[1] They thus create a retrospective discontinuity as well. They detach themselves from their natural ancestors. They live 'alone.' But they do have *spiritual* parents in their *gerontes* (elders), and may acquire *spiritual* children. They become members of the great family of God. "The monk is he who is detached from all, yet joined to all."[2]

Christ urges the faithful to call no man father on this earth: "And call no man your father upon the earth: for one is your

---

[1] See John Climacus, *The Ladder of Divine Ascent* 3,9, PG88D.
[2] Nilus the Ascetic (Evagrius of Pontus), *On Prayer* 124, PG79,1193C.

Father, which is in heaven."[3] No one except God can rightfully be called father. Yet at the same time, God is he "of whom all fatherhood in heaven and earth is named."[4] This means that any heavenly or earthly fatherhood finds meaning and acceptability insofar as it places itself within the perspective of the fatherhood of God and guides men to God.[5] Thus, biological kinship, which also ensures the biological continuity of the human race, is outstripped by spiritual kinship, which reveals itself at the same time on both a horizontal and a vertical level, and brings about the diachronic unity of the Church.

The diachronic unity of the Church, on the historical level, is expressed in apostolic succession. All bishops are successors of the Apostles in the unbroken line that is created by the canonical conferment and acceptance of the mystery of their consecration. At the same time, the Apostles and all bishops are as a 'type' of God.[6] Thus, from the point of view of history, where the variable of time interposes itself, the assurance of the preservation of the continuity is invested in the notion of apostolic succession, which ensures the unity of tradition. On the vertical plane, however, where time is set aside, the guarantee is placed in the truth of the symbolic relationship.

Christ is the leader and head of the Church. He it is, "which is, and which was, and which is to come."[7] The bishop, as successor of the Apostles and symbol of the presence of God, receives from God the gift of Christ and bestows it on the faithful by the grace of the Holy Spirit. Communion with God is not disrupted by time, but unity is realized in the Body of Christ—the Church. The historical perspective is assumed with the symbolic relationship and manifested as direct spiritual presence.

Apostolicity, which is safeguarded in the Church by the presence of the bishops, is not something which concerns them alone, but also the Church as a whole. The one, holy, catholic

---

[3]Matt. 23:9.
[4]Eph. 3:15.
[5]See G. Mantzaridis, *Orthodoxi pnevmatiki zoi*, Thessaloniki 1986, p.66.
[6]See Ignatius of Antioch, *To the Magnesians* 6,1; *To the Trallians* 3,1.
[7]Rev. 1:4.

Church of Christ is also *apostolic*. All the Orthodox Churches, from the point of view of history, are extensions of more ancient apostolic Churches. And all the Orthodox Churches, from the point of view of faith and life, preserve their apostolicity with their apostolic faith and their apostolic spirit.

A characteristic mark of the apostolic spirit is complete abandonment of self to God, the culmination of which is to be found in virginity. Virginity is not a state that concerns simply the body, but rather the body and soul as a whole. It is that state of "not living according to the flesh."[8] It is an unconditional contract of spiritual marriage with Christ. Bodily virginity of itself makes no sense; but it does have a very deep spiritual meaning when understood as an ally in the spiritual marriage.[9] To say 'yes' to biological discontinuity in order to exercise the virtue of virginity, represents the most radical form of commitment to the spiritual marriage with Christ. Thus, virginity, man's complete abandonment of himself to God, is the greatest gift that a man can offer to God.[10]

The Apostles of Christ, even those who were married at the time of their calling, left everything for Christ. There were many Christians of the first centuries who did the same. The Christian apologist Athenagoras states: "You will find many among us, both men and women, who have grown old without entering into marriage, in the hope of rather being joined with God."[11] The acceptance of Christianity as the official state religion, which gave rise to a certain secularization in the life of the Church and a waning of her charismatic elements, led to the flowering of monasticism and the transference of the center of the spiritual life of the faithful from the 'world' to the desert. At the same time, virginity, or at least celibacy, was established as a customary mark of the episcopate. Bishops

---

[8] See Gregory the Theologian, *Oration* 37,10, PG36,296A.

[9] "Perhaps the man who dares to say that bodily virginity is an ally of the internal spiritual marriage, will not be venturing something that is very far from what is probable." Gregory of Nyssa, *On Virginity* 19, PG46,397A.

[10] "For I am forever convinced that the greatest and finest offering and gift that it is in man's power to offer to God, and of which there is no compare, is the prize of virginity." Methodios, *Symposium* 5,1,PG18,97A.

[11] *Presbeia* 33.

began to be chosen from among the ranks of the monks, and the monasteries became centers for the development of the spiritual life and for training of the spiritual leaders of the Church.

Two questions arise as a result of the above: (a) What is the significance of the monastic life for the tradition of the Church, and (b) How does it contribute to the correct preservation and handing down of that tradition?

There are two elements in the Church's tradition: the historical and the purely spiritual. The historical element provides the guidelines, while the spiritual provides movement and life. The historical element is safeguarded by the institutions of the Church, while the spiritual element is served by the gifts of the Holy Spirit and by spiritual experience. The whole of the Church's life is guided by the Spirit of God, who imparts to man the gift of Christ without being confined by space and time.

The Church does not function with the historical factor alone, on the institutional level. She also needs the spiritual element that confirms her nature as communion of deification. This is why the leaders of the Church, the bishops, have not only an institutional, but also a charismatic position. Among the bishops, but working with them too, are also the charismatic figures—the saints. All bishops, as guarantors of the spiritual continuity in the life of the Church, are *called* saints, even if they are not saints. All saints guarantee the spiritual continuity of the life of the Church, even if they are not bishops. The disciple and biographer of St. Symeon the New Theologian, Nikitas Stethatos, in setting out the chief qualities a bishop should possess, sums them up as follows: The bishop is a man who has been cleansed of all ignorance by his sharing in the Holy Spirit, has been illumined richly by the brilliant brightness of the Holy Spirit, has gone on to achieve that perfection of which Christ is the measure, and has matured and acquired the mind of Christ in the science of the 'thearchic' communion.[12] Whoever, then, possesses these qualities, adds

---

[12]*Theoria kai synodos iera eis tin ouranion kai tin ekklisiastikin ierarchian* 35, Nikitas Stethatos, *Secret Works*, ed. by P. Chrestou, Thessaloniki 1957, p. 78.

Nikitas Stethatos, is a true bishop, "even though he has not been consecrated bishop and hierarch by men," yet belongs to the order of priests, deacons or monks. On the other hand, the bishop who has none of them, "is, in fact, an impostor, even though he thinks highly of himself by virtue of his consecration, and lords it over everyone else by virtue of his office, and sneers at them and exalts himself."[13]

The secularization of the life of the Church and the shift in emphasis of the episcopate from the charismatic to the administrative sphere, made the need for the presence of saints in the work of preserving and upholding the spiritual life of the faithful all the more intense. In this work, monasticism's contribution is decisive. While the world holds to a horizontal course, and the faithful try—with all the commitments and diversions of the world—to keep within the limits of ecclesiastical tradition, monasticism turns in another direction: the vertical. It strives to effect an emergence, an exodus from the world, setting its sights on the kingdom of God. This, moreover, is also the aim of the Church.

The members of the Church are not born as a result of the natural necessity of man to perpetuate the human race, but as a direct result of the will of God: "Which were born, not of blood, nor of the will of the flesh, nor of the will of man, but of God."[14] This birth introduces a spiritual scission into the biological continuity which opens up for men the prospect of union in Christ. All believers, whether married or unmarried, are saved by means of the spiritual marriage which they enter into with Christ in the Church, which is his virginal Body, deriving from the Virgin. Thus, while physical marriage serves to perpetuate the human race, spiritual marriage serves to render the human person indestructible in the communion of deification. The truth of this reveals itself in daily life in proportion to the spiritual progress of the faithful. As long as I am imperfect and disobedient, writes St. Maximos the Confessor, disobeying God by failing to keep his commandments and to

---

Cf. also Dionysios the Areopagite, *On the heavenly hierarchy* 7,3, PG3,209C.
 [13]Op. cit. 37, p. 79.
 [14]Jn. 1:13.

perfect myself spiritually, then Christ too is considered by men to be imperfect and disobedient because of me; for I diminish and mutilate Christ when I fail to increase in spirit with him as a member of his Body.[15]

This unifying scission, which is introduced into human life by regeneration in Christ, finds its most perfect expression in virginity. The perpetuation of death is severed by virginity. St. Gregory of Nyssa says that, in the body of the virgin, the whole chain of deaths which began with the first man and has continued until him, is sundered. Here we see too the meaning of the birth of Christ from the Virgin Mary. Christ, by virtue of his birth from the Virgin Mary (whose virginity signals the end of that death which held sway over the whole line of her ancestors), is no longer party to that inherited liability to death which is the lot of every man who is born according to the laws of nature.

Physical marriage and the natural line of succession offer man a constant and forever-repeated series of annihilations. This sort of marriage is tested by time and annihilated by death. We only approach the truth about physical marriage when we begin to transcend it. The more marriage is transferred from the physical to the spiritual plane, the closer we get to the truth about it as a communion of persons. But the natural succession of generations, which perpetuates the human race, is also being constantly annihilated by the death of the individual. We only approach the truth about man's existence when we begin to transcend our biological individuality. The more man shifts from biological necessity to spiritual freedom, the more he realizes his true worth as a human being, he distances himself from the vanity of the world and acquires a sense of the "age to come."[16]

Virginity is not at loggerheads with marriage. On the contrary, it is actually the highest form of marriage. It is that spiritual marriage which is not in the end annihilated, and consequently does not suppress the *eros* of man, but strengthens and perfects it. The voluntary deprivation which a man or

---

[15]*Chapters on Theology and Economy* 2,30, PG90,1137D-1140A.
[16]Isaac the Syrian, *Homily* 23.

woman undergoes on the immediate level renders possible the limitless fullness which lies beyond it. Thus, marriage holds a unique perspective in Christian life. The Christian is called to choose not so much between marriage and celibacy as between two different forms of marriage, the carnal and the spiritual. Of course, carnal marriage too, when entered into in Christ by the grace of the Holy Spirit, is also spiritual at the same time. But the spiritual marriage which moves beyond the limitations of biological necessity and is nourished by the experience of communion with God, has clearly an ecclesiological meaning.

The Spirit of God exists and acts in the Church. He guides her to all truth,[17] and while human defilement renders the communion of the Holy Spirit impossible,[18] purity, which culminates in virginity, attracts divine grace. It guarantees the preservation and continuance of the spiritual life of the Church, covering the Church, becoming her cloak.[19] Without the monastic life, which through virginity cultivates the spiritual dimension of the Church's tradition, there is no guarantee of the spiritual continuance of the life of the Church as communion between God and man.

---

[17]See Jn. 16:13.

[18]See Gregory Palamas, *Answer to Akindynos* 5, 27, 118, in *Syggrammata*, ed. P. Chrestou, vol. 3, Thessaloniki 1970, p. 377.

[19]John Chrysostom, *Commentary on Psalms* 44,12, PG55,202.

Chapter Eight

The Transfiguration Of Time

Time, just like the world with which it coexists and coextends, has more than one meaning for man. Just as the 'world'— as a world of decay and apostasy in thrall to sin and the devil—has a negative sense, so too time, as coextensive with the rule of sin and the devil that leads to decay and death, also has a negative sense. But on the other hand, just as the world as God's creation and object of divine providence has a positive meaning, so too does time, which coexists and coextends with the world in accordance with the will of the Creator have a positive meaning. Moreover in Christ, in whom man and the whole of creation are recapitulated and transfigured, time too is recapitulated and transfigured, serving the salvation and renewal of man and the whole world.

St. Gregory of Nyssa, referring to the mutability of human nature which man takes to be something fearful, observes that at the same time it affords him the only potential he has for acquiring perfection and his true worth. In St. Gregory's perspective, mutability, which is associated with man's physical and moral decay, becomes transfigured into a factor for "change towards that which is more excellent."[1] This is also the wider vision of the Church with respect to man and his life. Within the Church man is brought not to extinction but to

---

[1] *On Perfection*, PG 46,285C. W. Jaeger, *Gregorii Nysseni, Opera*, vol. VII,I, Leiden 1952, p. 213.

perfection, and his life is not destroyed but achieves its true value. Time is transfigured from a measure of decay and destruction to a measure of progress and perfection. Mutability changes from being a factor for dissolution to being a "kind of wing of flight to greater things."[2]

A real transfiguration of time is thus not comprehensible without the transfiguration of that mutability with which it also coexists. And since mutability, and with it time, determine man and his life, their transfiguration is actually brought about by the transfiguration of man and human life. It is brought about by man's ontological renewal and the change of this mutability from a course leading towards decay and death to a course leading towards regeneration and perfection. The issue has already become theological rather than anthropological. The change of mutability into a course leading towards regeneration and perfection is only possible with the assistance of powers which are beyond man and are to be found beyond that mutability and time that determine his existence. This is the transfiguration of man in Christ, and together with him, the entire world.

This transfiguration is not brought about solely by God, but presupposes the cooperation of man too. It requires his wholehearted dedication to the new life that Christ has presented to the world. As St. Maximos the Confessor puts it: "All visible realities need the Cross, that is, the state in which they are cut off from things acting upon them through the senses. All intelligible realities need burial, that is, the total quiescence of the things that act upon them through the intellect."[3] If a man does not crucify his natural movements and bury his thoughts, he will be unable to see the truth. Since it is without these prerequisites that man would remain forever far from the truth, the Church places before us the Cross and the Burial of Christ.

With the Cross and Burial of Christ are crucified and buried every worldly thought and every worldly idea. At the same

---

[2]Op. cit.
[3]Maximos the Confessor, *Chapters on Theology and Economy* 1,67, PG 90,1108B (trans. by Palmer, Sherrard and Ware in *Philokalia*, Faber & Faber).

time, however, the Cross and Burial of Christ create a new perspective and an indissoluble truth: the perspective of immortal life and the truth of eternal gladness. By joining his life and his lifetime to Christ, man transfigures them. His life becomes Christlike and his time acquires limitless dimensions.

The life of the Christian with these new properties and dimensions is admirably described by St. Nicholas Cabasilas in his work *On the Life in Christ*. This work begins with the statement that: "The life in Christ originates in this life and arises from it. It is perfected, however, in the life to come, when we shall have reached that last day."[4] The life in Christ is neither limited to the present, nor pushed into the future. Christ himself said, "My kingdom is not of this world."[5] He did not say, "My kingdom is not *in* this world." The present life and the life of the world to come are not to be put in separate compartments. They are organically linked. The kingdom of God which was revealed to the world in Christ, is not a distinct or autonomous kingdom, but the one uncreated and eternal kingdom of God. Time is linked to eternity and forms with it a continuum which has its foundation and fulfillment in Christ.

The life in Christ, which is nurtured by the Christian's placing himself and then keeping himself within the Body of Christ, exists in both the present age and the age to come; "and neither the present age can perfect it in the souls of men, nor the age to come, if it does not begin from here."[6] The life in Christ, like Christ, transcends time. But again, just as Christ, who transcends time, is present *in* it, so the life in Christ exists and reveals itself within time.

The relationship between the present life and the life to come is similar to the relationship between life in the womb and life after birth. Just as the embryo, during its gestation, is being prepared and formed in a dark place for the life that it is to live in the light of the world, so too are the saints prepared and formed during their earthly lives in accordance with the

---

[4]*On the Life in Christ* 1, PG 150,493B (trans. by deCatanzaro, St. Vladimir's Seminary Press).
[5]Jn. 18:36.
[6]*On the Life in Christ* 1, PG 150,493B.

life that awaits them in the light of the kingdom of God. However, while embryos do not acquire any sense of the life for which they are being prepared because this is solely and exclusively in the future and does not reveal itself at all in the place of their preparation, the saints already have in the present some experience of the life to come.[7]

The future of the faithful, which is none other than Christ himself, is not found *after* the present, but imbues and envelops the present as it does the past, because Christ himself is eternally present. St. Nicholas Cabasilas says that the life to come is "as it were, infused into this present life and mingled with it. For us too that Sun has graciously risen, the heavenly fragrance has been poured forth into the malodorous places, and the Bread of angels has been given even to men."[8]

It is said of St. Silouan, "His prayer reached out beyond the bounds of time, and all thought of the transitory phenomena of human life vanished . . . the mind in an act of intuitive synthesis being aware of everything simultaneously."[9] Here we have not a repudiation, but rather a transfiguration of time. The man of faith does not reject even the smallest particle of time, "and cannot even for a second forget the Lord."[10] So it is that eternity exists within time, while at the same time enveloping it and creating a new reality where temporal dimensions are transcended and the fullness of the life in Christ is made manifest.

Eternity has no duration, despite the fact that it encompasses the vast dimensions of the ages and of worldly time. Eternity can be described as "an eternal instant," which is not subject to definition or measurement.[11] And since it is not subject to definition or measurement, it is always present, but also always limitless and inexhaustible.

In the final analysis, only eternity is real. Time is nonexistent, and the only moment of time that is offered to man—the imperceptible moment of the present—is an image

---

[7]Op. cit., PG 150,496B.
[8]Op. cit. (trans. by deCatanzaro).
[9]Archimandrite Sophrony, *Saint Silouan the Athonite*, Essex 1991, pp. 48-49.
[10]Op. cit., p. 271.
[11]Archimandrite Sophrony, *We Shall See Him As He Is*, Essex 1988, p. 108.

The Transfiguration of Time

of eternity. Just as man exists "in the image" of God, so time exists "in the image" of eternity; and just as man has no hypostasis without the hypostasis of Divinity, so time has no hypostasis without eternity. Yet the man who is assumed into the hypostasis of the Divine Logos is saved, and time is transfigured for him into the *kairos* of salvation.[12]

Man exists always as a member of a wider community. Moreover, man has a past, which has its roots far beyond his own personal history. This past in various ways determines the present. Even more so, man's past from a biological, psychological, or even social point of view, coincides to a great extent with his present. From this standpoint, man can be seen as a slave of his past.

Yet at the same time, man has the capacity to differentiate himself from his past. He can adopt a critical, or even a negative attitude towards it. Thus his life in the present can constitute an organic continuation of his past, but it could also be a real refutation of the past. This continuation or refutation is effected not only according to the way in which he deals with the present, but also according to the way in which he views his past. The past, of course, exists as a datum which cannot of itself change. Nevertheless, although it may not of itself change, a man's attitude to it may change, and this is of decisive importance in his life. The lost past is reassessed in the present, while he dissociates himself from it and goes on to a new life. Yet any dissociation from the past is purely conventional, and any renewal of life is relative. While mutability leads to decay, real renewal is impossible, and while death breaks down life, the true freedom of man is unattainable.

Finally, man lives with hope for the future. Moreover, freedom is expressed by reaching forward into the future. The future, which is presented as indeterminable, itself determines, according to Sartre, not only the present but also the past. It decides whether the past is to live or die.[13] The decision about the future, however, is either taken in the present or postponed indefinitely. In the first instance, the future too becomes

---
[12] Cf. 2 Cor. 6:2.
[13] J.P. Sartre, *L'être et le néant*, Paris 1943, p. 580.

present. In the second instance, the future remains nonexistent. Moreover, man's future is neither limitless nor free from obligations. His time of life is limited and the fear of death is always with him.

We confront the past, then, as well as the future, in the present. The past is approached through memory, the future through expectation. Memory and expectation operate in the present and survive as long as man himself survives. For something to exist in life, it has to be experienced as something in the present. Whatever is not experienced as present does not exist in human life, even if it did exist once or is about to exist as an objective realty. This is why the Church, too, constantly offers in the present the mystery of the economy* in Christ, which recapitulates and transforms the world.

It is worth remembering here St. Anthony according to whom progress in virtue and the ascetic life which is undertaken for that purpose, should not be measured in time but in desire and intention. The saint himself took no account of the time which passed, but every day made greater efforts to advance in the ascetic life as though he were only just beginning the struggle, constantly repeating St. Paul's saying: "Forgetting those things which are behind, and reaching forth unto those things which are before."[14] Mindful, moreover, of the words of the prophet Elijah, "As the Lord of Hosts liveth, before whom I stand, I will surely show myself unto him today,"[15] he emphasized the setting aside of the past and the concentration of all man's attention on the present.[16]

Man is called to be vigilant and to develop the gift which God offers him in the present.[17] Besides, this is the only certain element of time at his disposal. The negative elements of the past should not overshadow the efforts of the present, but nei-

---

Economy: a term in Orthodox theology which, in the present context, refers to the divine plan for the salvation of man.

[14]Phil. 3:13.
[15]1 Kings 18:15.
[16]Athanasios the Great, *Life of St. Anthony* 7, PG 26,853B.
[17]Cf. Heb. 3:7-13.

ther should its positive elements create a spirit of complacency. For this reason, the daily resumption of the spiritual struggle with eagerness and joy is the best rule if man's goal is to be realized.[18]

Man finds perfection and the fullness of his life in Christ. Before the coming of Christ, humanity was 'without a head' and without hypostasis. But with the Birth of Christ, who is the head of the Church, men are united and each becomes a true hypostasis. "It was the birth of the head which brought the members into existence. If, then, birth is the beginning of life for a person, so that to be born is to begin one's life, and Christ is the life of those who cleave to him, then they were born when Christ entered this life and was born into it."[19] The faithful are joined in the hypostasis of Christ, thereby winning their true selves and transfiguring their allotted time of life.

The transfiguration of man's allotted time of life comes about with the "putting on" of the life in Christ. Participation in the life of Christ lends a new character and content to the time of life of the man of faith. His progress towards the future does not remain aimless and vague, but acquires a specific content and goal. The Christian shares in a new life and has a specific purpose to his life—that of progress and perfection in Christ. With his faith and hope in Christ, he becomes a communicant of eternity and awaits the final revelation of this new life which he already experiences "in part" in the present life.

The way we deal with the past is similar. More specifically, the transfiguration of the past is effected by repentance. Repentance is not just a single act of man, but an entire way of life. Repentance restores man to the real framework of his existence, placing him in the time of the Church, which is time of remembrance of God. It brings him from the alienation which arises from disobedience back into "fellowship with God."[20] Repentance does not mean the *repudiation* of the past, but its *transfiguration* and *winning over* to another perspective

---

[18]"Do thou therefore always begin the work of God with joy and eagerness." Isaac the Syrian, *Homily* 56.

[19]Nicholas Cabasilas, *On the Life in Christ* 4, PG 150,604A (trans. by deCatanzaro).

[20]Basil the Great, *On the Holy Spirit* 15,35, PG 32,128D.

which the Death and Resurrection of Christ have opened up for the world. Repentance turns the negative content of the past, sin, into the means of achieving perfection. It becomes, as one ascetic put it, dung for the cultivation of virtue. In this way we manage to achieve a creative view, a transfiguration, of the past.

On the other hand, hope in Christ, which through communion in the mysteries acquires a substantial foundation and is turned into a certain expectation, transfigures the future. This expectation has an eschatological character and awaits its fulfillment in the kingdom of God. St. Nicholas Cabasilas points out that for the saints, the future is already present in this life, but its presence is not full and complete, as it will be in the life to come.[21]

As with the Christian faith, so in the Christian life, human limitations are swept aside and with them the restricting principles of human logic. The belief that Christ is at the same time God and man transcends the fundamental logical principle of identity and contradiction. In common logic everything is identified with itself and cannot be something different from itself. A is A. It cannot at the same time be A and 'not A.' However, that which at a given point of time is A, can later become 'not A.' The intervention of time justifies this contradiction. What happens, however, when the time factor is eliminated?[22] How many restrictions disappear, and how many contradictions become unjustifiable?

Christ, who is perfect man, is also perfect God, and although he lived as man in a specific time and place in the world, he existed and exists as God everywhere and always. He is "he which is, and which was, and which is to come."[23] As God-man he exists in time, but he also transcends time. He is

---

[21]"For if that which is in the future is present with them while they yet live in the body, they already experience the prize, yet not continually or perfectly, since this life does not permit it. For this cause 'we rejoice in hope' . . . For 'always' looks to the future only." *On the Life in Christ* 7, PG 150,724B (trans. by deCatanzaro).

[22]Cf. R. Panikkar, "Die Zukunft kommt nicht später," *Vom Sinn der Tradition*, ed. L. Reinish, Munich 1970, pp. 56-57.

[23]Rev. 1:8.

to be found in any place we might mention, but he is not confined to any particular place.

What happens, however, when with the life in Christ, the life of Christ becomes the life of man too? What happens when the eternity of Christ's life is joined to human temporality? In this event, time now loses for man too its restrictive power. Many contradictions disappear. That which goes before does not oppose that which comes afterwards. The means do not conflict with the end. The things of the present are joined to those of the past and the future. The 'now' becomes 'forever.'

All the faithful share in the life of Christ in proportion to their purity and their receptivity. The many become one and the one many. The glory of Christ, in which his human nature too took part from the beginning, is offered to the faithful according to the measure of their purity. Mortals become immortal, and men of clay become spirit-bearers. Limitations of time are set aside and bonds are loosed.

The power which lifts the temporal and wider restrictions of man and loosens his bonds is Christ himself. For this reason, a precondition for their transcendence and the transfiguration of man's life is his entering into the life of Christ. The righteous of the Old Testament are not essentially different from other men of their times, save for the preparations they have made, and the longing they have experienced, to receive Christ. If then they are called righteous and friends of God, then this appellation is a conventional one, since they prepared themselves to have recourse to righteousness when this presented itself, and to see the light when this appeared, and to move on from the formalities of the law to the truth when this revealed itself.[24]

Yet with the transcendence of temporal distinctions, the essential distinction between means and end, as we have already said, is also removed. The present, which is usually thought of as the means for realizing future aims, is itself offered for the immediate realization of aims, because it already includes the future in it too. And the future, which already exists in the present, makes any puzzling conflict between means and end superfluous. The means exist together

---

[24]Nicholas Cabasilas, *On the Life in Christ* 1, PG 150,508D.

with the end. And the end is offered at the same time also as the means for its realization. Faith is identified with hope, and hope gives foundation to the content of faith in the same present: "Now faith is the substance of things hoped for, the evidence of things not seen."[25] The life in Christ is not a means of acquiring the kingdom of God, but the kingdom of God itself is as a pledge within the present. And the awaited kingdom of God is not the aim of the life in Christ, but the life in Christ itself in its full revelation.[26]

The man of faith lives the presence of the kingdom of God in the world by means of his participation in the mystery of the Holy Eucharist. When he takes part in this mystery not only with his physical but also with his spiritual senses, he is united with the God-man, Christ. He becomes a communicant of his glory and his divinity.[27] His whole life thus becomes one ceaseless celebration. The passage of time in his life is transfigured into a passage "from the visible to the intelligible," where shadows and symbols cease and the eternal truth is revealed.[28]

An important means of preserving this communion with Christ and the revelation of his grace, is the invocation of his name. This invocation, which is made by means of this short prayer, "Lord Jesus Christ, Son of God, have mercy upon me," is also called "the indwelling of Jesus Christ."[29] By the constant repetition of this prayer, the man of faith receives Christ within him. He makes the life of Christ his life, and imparts the perspective of eternity to his time. He interweaves time with eternity, and thus he transfigures time.

---

[25] Heb. 11:1.
[26] See 1 Jn. 3:2.
[27] "It is only those who, in partaking of the divine flesh of the Lord are being made worthy also, by close noetic contact of the revelation of the invisible divinity which they see and eat with the eye and the mouth of the mind, that know that Christ is the Lord. They do not simply eat the bread which is sensible in a way that is sensible, but they also eat at the same time God, whom they eat and drink in a way that is noetic, so that, fed at once by both the visible and the invisible in their similarly double senses, they unite themselves in both ways to Christ who also has two natures, fused as they are with him and sharing in his glory and his divinity." Symeon the New Theologian, *Ethical Discourses* 14, 233-241, ed. J. Darrouzes, *Sources Chrétiennes*, vol. 129, Paris 1967, p. 438.
[28] See op. cit., 282-284.
[29] Symeon of Thessaloniki, *On Divine Prayer* 296, PG 155, 544D.

Chapter Nine

Liturgical Time

The Church with her feasts and services actuates the work of divine economy within time, thereby sanctifying and transforming the time of everyday life. At the same time, she integrates it with, and directs it towards, its eschatological fulfillment—the kingdom of God.

The Church's feasts, preeminent among which are the feasts of the Lord, are not mere commemorations. They are opportunities—*kairoi* for communion with Christ and the Church. This communion, which is brought about "through the intercessions of the saints and of the Theotokos," preserves the faithful and gives them increase within the body of the Church, offering them the gifts of divine economy. In following the annual cycle of feasts, the weekly festive cycle and the daily cycle of day and night offices, the faithful worshipper lives the whole work of divine economy and comes to share in the life of the kingdom of God even in this present life.

Distinction is made between the movable and fixed feasts of the Church. The immovable feasts are tied to a fixed date in the Church's year which begins on the first day of September. They present us with specific redemptive interventions of God in the history of man, or with historical persons and events in the life of the Church: the Annunciation, the Nativity of Christ, Theophany, the Transfiguration, feasts of the Theotokos, and the feasts of the angels and saints. These feasts serve to sanctify time and transform it in the light of the kingdom of God.

The movable feasts constitute a special sequence which stands apart from historical time and guides man above and beyond it. Fashioning a new dimension of time as though suspended above that temporality to which history is subject, it thus offers limitless vistas to the man who is shackled by time. At the center of the movable feasts is Pascha, the "feast of feasts." Pascha not only determines the period of preparation that begins with the Triodion,* and the period of Pentecost that follows it, but it affects the whole of the liturgical year. It is around Pascha, as though around a central axis, that all the Sundays of the Church's year are determined liturgically and numbered. While the fixed feasts, like the Annunciation and Christmas, bear witness to the advent of the eternal into time, the movable feasts, like Pascha or the Ascension, affirm the transition from time to eternity.

In the final analysis all the feasts of the Church, the fixed and the movable, are recapitulated in one movable feast, Pascha, which is the feast of the passage of the faithful from this world into the kingdom of God. Pascha has no fixed date in time. In the mystery of Pascha, which is also the mystery of Great and Holy Friday and Pentecost, the believer celebrates his regeneration in Christ and his incorporation into the world of eternity.[1]

The Church lives the mystery of divine economy at different levels: over a long period of time, or *macrochronically* (in the annual cycle), and over a short period, or *microchronically* (in the weekly and daily cycles). The liturgical time of the Church is flexible and multidimensional. It both stretches over the whole of the calendar year, and is contracted into each individual week and day. It is set forth at length in festivals that cover an extended period of time, and summarized in

---

Triodion—liturgical service book 'of three odes,' which contains the variable parts of the Lenten and the Paschal cycle of services.

---

[1] See Origen, *Contra Celsus* 8,21-22, PG11, 1549C-1552B.

short festivals that are confined to a few days or hours, to be recapitulated finally in the Divine Liturgy.

Macrochronic celebration

Macrochronic celebration takes place primarily in the cycle of movable feasts with Pascha at their heart. Ten weeks before Pascha the period of the Triodion begins. The first three weeks of the Triodion constitute an introduction to Great Lent that follows, and prepares us for the main purpose of Lent, repentance: "Open wide the gates of repentance O Life-giver . . ."[2] This introduction begins with the Sunday of the Publican and the Pharisee, continues with the Sundays of the Prodigal Son and Meatfare, and ends with the Sunday of Cheesefare. The eve of the Sunday of Meatfare, on which is read the gospel passage concerning the Last Judgement, is dedicated to those who have fallen asleep in Christ. It is called Memorial Saturday. Finally there is Cheesefare Sunday, which is also called the Sunday of Forgiveness, and is dedicated to the memory of 'the expulsion of Adam from Paradise.'

The period of Great Lent which follows and lasts for seven weeks, is a symbol of our present life as expectation of, and striving for, communion with Christ. The man of faith contemplates the pain that arises from the Fall, and repents. He strives to shake off his enslavement to this world and to live that freedom that God offers. Great Lent is the arena of that struggle. The repentance that sets men free from enslavement to the world and from the tyranny of their own selfish pride demands much effort. It should not be an empty show, but rather an actual way of life.

Fasting is not an end in itself but a *means* to an end. It must be accompanied by humility, prayer, love and charitable works. Man is not to follow his own will, but to subordinate it to the rule of the Church. If the power of the devil is to be overcome, prayer and fasting are necessary.[3] But fasting also helps us to win self control: "Rule your stomach, before it rules you."[4]

---

[2] Troparion, Sunday Matins of the Triodion.
[3] See Matt. 17:21.
[4] John Climacus, *The Ladder of Divine Ascent* 14,4, PG88,865D.

The Fathers of the Church point out that the first commandment that God gave man while yet in Paradise was the commandment to fast: "Of every tree of the garden thou mayest freely eat; but of the tree of the knowledge of good and evil, thou shalt not eat of it: for in the day that thou eatest thereof thou shalt surely die."[5] But man did not obey this command and was exiled from Paradise. Christ, the new Adam, began his work with a fast. And when the Devil tempted him, he replied, "Man shall not live by bread alone."[6] In his preparations for his return to Paradise, to the kingdom of God, the Christian imitates Christ by fasting in body and in spirit, from food and from sin.

It is by means of fasting that man activates his spiritual nature, his unique calling as man. Our experience of the ravages of the consumer society helps us to understand also the practical consequences of fasting.

Finally, Great Lent, as St. Dorotheos points out, takes up one-tenth of the lifetime of the faithful. The seven weeks of this period, if one takes out the Saturdays and Sundays, amount to a total of fast days which corresponds to one tenth of the days of the year. Thus, just as the Israelites offered to God the tenth part of their possessions so that all their works might be blessed, so do Christians offer the tenth part of their time so that there may be a blessing on their works, and that they may be shown mercy throughout the year.[7]

The Sundays of Great Lent are dedicated to persons and things that lend support to the faithful in their spiritual struggle. The first Sunday in Lent is dedicated, for historical and symbolic reasons, to Orthodoxy. Right belief is the foundation of the spiritual life. There then follow the Sundays of the great ascetics of Orthodoxy, St. Gregory Palamas, St. John of the Ladder, and finally of St. Mary of Egypt. In the middle of the period of fasting is the Sunday of the Veneration of the Cross: "We are like those following a long and cruel path, who become tired, see a beautiful tree with many leaves, sit in its

---

[5]Gen. 2:16-17.
[6]Matt. 4:4.
[7]*Discourses* 15. 1. PG88,1788BC.

shade and rest for awhile and then, as if rejuvenated, continue their journey; likewise today, in the time of fasting and difficult journey and effort, the life-giving Cross was planted in our midst by the holy fathers to give us rest and refreshment, to make us light and courageous for the remaining task."[8] The Cross is the symbol of the Christian life, of a life of dedication to God, and of freedom in Christ. This is why the faithful are constantly reminded of that humility which rendered the Publican's prayer acceptable, while at the same time the hypocrisy of the Pharisee is censured.

The Fathers of the Church liken Great Lent to the forty-year journey of Israel through the desert before they reached the promised land. The liturgical structure of Great Lent too creates a sense of expectation of the salvation which is in Christ. The number of readings from the Old Testament increases; yet the Old Testament leads us to Christ, who came in order to save the world.

In times past, Great Lent was specially devoted to the preparation of catechumens for Baptism and the Eucharist, although the faithful too had the opportunity of living again the mystery of their entry into the Church. "Great is the tyranny of forgetfulness," says St. Nicholas Cabasilas.[9] The man of faith needs to be reminded of, and to live again and again, the mystery of his salvation and restoration, lest he be beguiled by oblivion. The Orthodox Church preserves, even in our day when ordinarily there are no catechumens, forms and elements from the *typicon* (or rite) of the Liturgy which refer to the catechumens.

And then, as the culmination of Great Lent, comes Holy Week. The man who has endured the toil of fasting, and exerted himself in humility, love, repentance and prayer, is now called to live Christ's Passion and Resurrection with him, for it is these that initiate us into the spiritual marriage with Christ the Bridegroom, and bring us into his heavenly kingdom.

The offices of the first three days are usually referred to as the services of the Bridegroom. On Holy Wednesday, the cus-

---

[8]*Synaxaristis* for the Sunday of the Veneration of the Cross.
[9]*Commentary on the Divine Liturgy* 21, PG150,413C.

tom in the Orthodox Church is to celebrate the mystery of Holy Unction. This sacrament can be celebrated on any other day of the year as well, either in church or in the houses of the faithful, principally for the benefit of those who are sick. Man is an integral union of soul and body, and illness is not simply a physical, but also a spiritual disorder. All the faithful have need of the blessing bestowed by the sacrament. The Orthodox Church offers Holy Unction in conjunction with the whole of the faithful's rite of preparation for the Holy Eucharist, and the celebration of Holy Unction on Holy Wednesday, on the eve of the commemoration of the Last Supper, is an excellent demonstration of this.

The Last Supper, at which the mystery of the Holy Eucharist is handed down to us, is celebrated on Holy Thursday. The custom is to include in this celebration the washing of the feet of the priests by the bishops; "Ye know that the princes of the Gentiles exercise dominion over them, and they that are great exercise authority upon them. But it shall not be so among you: but whosoever will be great among you, let him be your minister; and whosoever will be chief among you, let him be your servant."[10]

Christ did not die on the Cross so that his followers might live a life of ease, but so that they might imitate him and free themselves, by toil and suffering, from sin. In this way they will be able to live a new life as resurrected men and women. However, they cannot rise again if they do not first die.

Death is more powerful than human life. But he who dies with Christ, dies within the hypostasis of true life which is stronger than death and has conquered death. Christ, who is eternally present, is the *locus* of the eternal presence of man, he is the "land of the living." This is why the Church can pledge eternal memory to the dead.

Man is not limited to his biological existence. His life is not the same as his lifetime. Transcending his own individuality, he draws near to his fellow man, and in the person of his neighbor he sees Christ, who has conquered death.

---

[10]Matt. 20:25-27.

Liturgical Time

On Holy and Great Friday, the Resurrection is already beginning to emerge. It is the custom for the children to pass underneath the epitaphion (the burial shroud of Christ*), which stands decked with flowers in the midst of the church. In many parishes, after the procession with the epitaphion, the priests hold it up high at the church door, so that the faithful can pass underneath it on their return to the church. This passing suggests a new birth. Out of the tomb of Christ, the new man is born. It is a symbolic participation in the Death of Christ, whose Death brings forth the Resurrection. It constitutes a reminder of the meaning of Christian Baptism. The man of faith always has to suffer, die and rise again with Christ not just once, but daily.

The culmination and central axis of the whole festive period is *Pascha*, or Easter—the passage from earth to heaven, from death to life: "The Day of Resurrection! Let us be illumined. O ye people! Pascha, Pascha of the Lord! From death unto life and from earth unto heaven hath Christ our God brought us over, singing a song of victory."[11] *Pascha* is "the feast of feasts and festival of festivals."[12] "We celebrate the death of Death, the annihilation of Hell, the beginning of a life new and everlasting."[13] At the Paschal Liturgy, in partaking of the Holy Eucharist, the believer partakes of the kingdom of God, while at the same time entreating that he may partake of the Lord "more perfectly . . . in the day which knoweth no night of thy kingdom."[14] The feast of the Resurrection is also a feast of love. At Vespers on the day of Pascha, which is called the Vespers of Love, the gospel passage is read out in several languages as a symbol of love and the reconciliation of nations.

Pascha is the beginning of a new period as regards the cycle of movable feasts—the period of the Pentecostarion. This lasts for eight weeks, and symbolizes the life to come. While in the

---

*The epitaphion depicts the crucified and buried Christ. It is placed upon the representation of the tomb of Christ and venerated by the faithful.

[11] Paschal Canon, Irmos of the first ode.
[12] Op. cit., Irmos of the eighth ode.
[13] Op. cit., Troparion of the seventh ode.
[14] Op. cit., Troparion of the ninth ode.

Old Testament, the exodus from Egypt (the Pascha) is completed by the giving of the Law on Mount Sinai, in the New Testament, the Christian Pascha is fulfilled by the gift of the Holy Spirit at Pentecost.[15] The Christian receives in his heart the Spirit of God and already in this life has a foretaste of the life to come. Amid the world of corruption, he lives the joy of the Resurrection.

Forty days after Pascha, we celebrate the Ascension of the Lord. The Ascension completes the work of the economy in Christ. Human nature is raised to the glory of God: "But God . . . even when we were dead in sins, hath quickened us together with Christ . . . and hath raised us up together, and made us sit together in heavenly places in Christ Jesus."[16]

Ten days after Ascension, that is on the seventh Sunday after Pascha, we celebrate Pentecost. The eve of this feast is dedicated to the dead as a Memorial Saturday. This is the second Memorial Saturday of the Church's year, and once again belongs to the cycle of movable feasts. The dead do not exist in the time that is of this world. They are already, even before the Last Judgement, in the age to come. The Church offers prayers for her children without ceasing, not only while they are alive, but after their death as well. On the day of Pentecost a litany is offered again for the souls of the dead.

Pentecost offers man the fruits of the redemptive and restorative work of Christ. Christ himself said to his disciples: "It is expedient for you that I go away; for if I go not away, the Comforter will not come unto you; but if I depart, I will send him unto you."[17] Pentecost is the day of the descent of the Holy Spirit, the day of the founding of the Church, of the fellowship of the children of God. This is why this Pentecostal hymn is also sung at the consecration of bishops: "The Holy Spirit bestows all things, brings forth prophecies, perfects priests, has taught wisdom to the unlettered, and made theologians of fishermen. He holds together the whole institution of the Church."[18]

---

[15]Cf. A. Schmemann, *I Ekklisia prosefchomeni*, Athens 1991, pp. 101-102.
[16]Eph. 2:4-6.
[17]John 16:7.
[18]Stichiron, Vespers of Pentecost.

Of course, the Church in her institutional form often dries up, and becomes transformed from the sphere where communion with God takes place, to a means of separating man from God. Where this situation arises, the Spirit is extinguished. But the Church in her essence is the sphere where the Holy Spirit manifests himself. She is the place of true freedom, of the freedom which transcends the world, decay and death: "And where the Spirit of the Lord is, there is liberty."[19] It is, according to the teaching of the Orthodox tradition, "the communion of deification."

Pentecost is the last great movable feast. And yet, the cycle of the feasts of Pentecost, and with it the whole sequence of movable feasts, does not come to an end with this feast, but with the feast of All Saints. The regenerative work of Christ, and in general all those things that happened as a result of his Death, Resurrection and Ascension, happened for the sanctification of man. This is why the feast of All Saints is placed at the end of the cycle of movable feasts as their culmination, representing the goal of history and divine economy, the symbol of the heavenly Jerusalem, the kingdom of God.

The feast of All Saints embraces the whole history of mankind. It links the present to the past and the future. It unites heaven and earth, time and eternity. On All Saints' day, as the *Synaxarion* of the Orthodox Church says, "we celebrate all those things which the Holy Spirit in his bounty sanctified ... the angelic hosts, the Forefathers and Patriarchs, the Prophets and the blessed Apostles, the Martyrs and the Hierarchs, the Hieromartyrs and the Monk-martyrs, the venerable and the just, and all the choirs of saintly women, and all those other saints whose names we know not, with whom stand also those yet to be born."

Apart from these movable feasts, which highlight, above all, the eschatological character of the Church and her passage from time to eternity, there are also, as we have seen, the immovable feasts, which stress the sanctification of time and the presence of the eternal within it. The Annunciation, the Nativity of Christ, Theophany, the feasts of the Theotokos and

---
[19] 2 Cor. 3:17.

the feasts of the angels and the saints stress above all the presence of eternity within time itself. Christ came into the world as Son of the Virgin. In the person of the Panagia, the preparation of mankind that was carried out chiefly in the Old Testament, became complete. Mary, with her complete humility and devotion to God, made the Incarnation of God possible: "Today is the crown of our salvation and the manifestation of the mystery that is from all eternity."[20] The feast of the Annunciation inaugurates the manifestation of the mystery of the Divine Incarnation.

At the same time, the Panagia, with her perfect humility and obedience to God, became the principle and model of the Christian life. For man has to do nothing except entrust himself to God, so that he may receive his saving and regenerative grace. There is nothing more for him to do in all his thoughts, his words, his actions and his whole moral conduct, than simply to sweep aside the obstacles and weaknesses to which his human nature is subject, and let the grace of God work within him.

In his life, a man has to confront evil and his own weaknesses, and needs to fight them if he is to win his release from them. If he abides in the will of God, he will win that freedom that delivers him from any form of domination, even from the domination of death. This is precisely the attitude of Christ, who as man, was completely obedient to the will of his Father. And it is the same attitude that the Panagia exhibits when she makes her reply to the Archangel. It is her absolute love of, and devotion to, God that constitute her true virginity and freedom. It was these that made the advent of Christ possible.

Christmas is the feast of the Incarnation of God: "He who holds the whole creation in the hollow of his hand today is born of the Virgin."[21] The unoriginate and timeless God is born within time as a man, in order to save mankind. The corruptible body that man acquired as a consequence of his fall, is regenerated by the Incarnation of God, so that the feast of the Incarnation of God is at the same time the feast of the deifica-

---

[20] Apolytikion of the Annunciation.
[21] Idiomelon of the Ninth Hour, Christmas.

tion of man. God became man so that he might deify man.[22] Deification is offered as the possibility for, and the final goal of, man from the moment of God's Incarnation; and our chronology begins from the Nativity of Christ. This is the decisive turning point in history. Man who wanted to become god but failed, now becomes god in Christ.

More ancient, but even more splendid than the feast of Christmas, is the feast of Theophany.[23] During the baptism of Christ in the Jordan by John, the Triune God is made manifest: "Today Christ has come to be baptized in the Jordan; today John touches the head of the Master."[24] Christ, who is baptized by John, is borne witness to as Son of God by the voice of the Father and the descent of the Holy Spirit in the form of a dove. This is what is meant by Theophany, the manifestation of the Holy Trinity. Anyone who believes in Christ is baptized in the name of the Holy Trinity. With his submersion in the water, the selfish, and therefore sinful man dies, while with his emergence from the water, the man made new in the freedom that is of God, is born. This new life is only possible with the grace of the Holy Spirit. And the Spirit acts in the communion of the faithful which is called the Church. The incorporation into this communion is completed by Chrismation which is performed immediately after Baptism.

Everything that a man does, his struggle against his love of self, his fight against the devil and evil, his pursuit of virtue and what is good, is all effected by the grace of the Holy Spirit. It is this grace that binds us to Christ and to the communion of the faithful. Moreover, each man bears Christ in his entirety within himself, so that he should be treated as though he were Christ himself, and not be thought of as an anonymous cipher

---

[22]See e.g. Athanasios the Great, *On the Incarnation of the Logos* 54,3, PG25,192B.

[23]"Joyful was the feast that has passed, glorious is the present day. On that day, the Magi worshipped the Saviour. On this day, a chosen servant baptizes the Master. Then, Shepherds dwelling in the fields saw and were amazed; Now, the voice of the Father proclaims his only-begotten Son." Doxastikon, Vespers for the Forefeast of the Theophany.

[24]Stichiron idiomelon, Lauds (the Praises) of the Theophany.

amidst a faceless gathering called a church. Man as person and member of the Church of Christ is an icon of the Triune God.

The Transfiguration has a central place and importance in the Orthodox Church. At his Transfiguration, Christ gave his three disciples the opportunity of seeing, insofar as a human being may, the glory of his divinity. The Transfiguration of Christ is at the same time a confirmation of his divinity and an intimation of his voluntary journey towards death. Although he is God, and can avoid death, he endures his Passion and Death as man. Once again the voice of the Father affirms the divinity of the Son, whom all men are called to obey. The Orthodox Church is the Church of the Transfiguration. This feast presages and affirms the renewal of creation. The whole cosmos, matter itself, is transfigured by the grace of God.

The glory of Christ which the disciples saw on Mount Tabor, was no fleeting phenomenon. It was the eternal light of his divinity which was communicated to man in Christ and is always manifested as a pledge of the contemplation of God, face to face.

Alongside these immovable feasts of Christ, there are also, as we have seen, the feasts of the Mother of God, which are all fixed, as are the feasts of the saints. The saints are members of the Body of Christ. Their feasts, each of which imparts its own particular character to the days of the year, sanctify time and transform it in the light of Christ. This is why each feast is completed from the Church's point of view by the celebration of the mystery of the Holy Eucharist and the communion of the faithful. This, the mystery of the Holy Eucharist, the Christian Pascha, sums up and recapitulates all the feasts of the Church, the movable and the fixed.

Microchronic celebration

Microchronic celebration, that is the celebration of the work of divine economy over short periods of time, is performed in the weekly cycle and in the daily offices.

In the Old Testament, the week represents the time taken for the creation of the world. Its seventh day, the Sabbath, is the day on which God rested. On the Sabbath, the Israelite shares in God's rest, and honors the creator of the world. The Church has preserved the notion of the week, but accorded it new content and orientation.

In the Church, the weekly cycle essentially preserves the character of the cycle of the year's movable feasts. The events celebrated are not associated with specific dates, but with the days of the week. Besides, many of the movable as well as the fixed feasts, which are given an extended celebration during the Church's year, are recapitulated in the weekly cycle as well. Monday is the day of the Bodiless Powers (the angelic hosts), Tuesday belongs to St. John the Baptist, Wednesday to the Panagia, Thursday to the Holy Apostles and St. Nicholas. Again, Wednesdays, Fridays and Saturdays in particular, by and large preserve the same character as they possess in the extended festival of Pascha during Holy Week. The Wednesday and Friday fasts are directly linked to the betrayal by Judas and the Crucifixion of Christ. Saturday (the Sabbath) has preserved in the Church too the same festive character that it had in the Old Testament, but has acquired new content as well. In addition to the rest from the work of creation, we now have rest from the work of cosmic regeneration. Saturday is, for the Church, the day "on which the Only-Begotten Son of God rested from all his works."[25] Thus, this day too assumes a marked liturgical character and is closely associated with the celebration of the Holy Eucharist. It is significant that during Great Lent, when the celebration of the Holy Eucharist is not permitted on weekdays, an exception is made for Saturdays.

But the day of festival *par excellence* for the Church is Sunday. In fact the whole festive cycle of the week is based on Sunday. Sunday is not just the first day of the week, the day of the commencement of creation; it is also the "eighth day," the day of Christ's Resurrection and the regeneration of the world. The Church does not celebrate the Resurrection only once a year, but every Sunday too. Sunday as the "eighth day," the day of the Resurrection, transcends time and brings us into

---

[25] Doxastikon, Matins of Holy Saturday.

eternity.[26] This is why it is the day above all others for the celebration of the Holy Eucharist.

At Sunday Matins, after the reading of the Resurrection Gospel, the hymn "Having beheld the Resurrection of Christ..." is proclaimed. St. Symeon the New Theologian points out that the hymn does not say that we have *believed* in the Resurrection of Christ, but that we have *seen* it, for the Resurrection becomes reality in the heart of every believer.[27] Thus, the Christian lives the Resurrection not only beyond, but also before, his physical death.

Finally, the cycle of the daily offices links the main points in these twenty-four hours with the essential landmarks in the work of divine providence. These points are the afternoon, the evening, midnight, the dawn, the first hour of the day, the third, sixth and ninth hours. It is with the office of the afternoon, i.e. Vespers, that the daily services commence. Vespers is associated particularly with the creation of the world, while Compline is associated with the remembrance of death.[28] The midnight office, the *mesonyktikon*, refers to the Resurrection and Second Coming of the Lord,[29] and Matins to the coming of Christ and the abolition of darkness in the world. The first hour, which is also a dawn hour, is associated chiefly with the manifestation of Christ as the true light which enlightens man. The third hour is the hour of the descent of the Holy Spirit on the day of Pentecost, as portrayed in the Acts of the Apostles.[30] The sixth hour is the hour of Christ's Crucifixion, and the ninth hour is the hour of his Death.

In the daily offices, the presence of God and of the work of his providence in the world are actualized in accordance with the symbolism of the different times of day. These offices have more in common with the immovable feasts in that they allow

---

[26] See Gregory of Nyssa, *Writings on the Psalms* 2,5, PG44,504D.

[27] *Catechetical Discourses* 13,97-100, ed. by B. Krivocheine, *Sources Chrétiennes*, vol. 104, Paris 1964, p. 198.

[28] See Symeon of Thessaloniki, *On Divine Prayer* 299-300, PG155,553AC.

[29] For more on this see A. Kalyvopoulos, *Chronos teleseos tis theias Leitourgias*, Thessaloniki 1982, p.81.

[30] See Acts 2:15.

eternity to break through into history. The events celebrated here are associated with specific hours of the day. But these offices too find their culmination and summation again in the Divine Liturgy, which is not determined by time, but itself determines time.

It is significant that the Divine Liturgy makes no particular reference to specific hours of the day or night, nor is it linked by its content exclusively to a certain period of time. It is free of the restraints of time and can in fact be performed at any time,[31] morning, afternoon or evening. Free from time, but also having the whole of time at his disposal, the man of faith experiences the 'blessed kingdom of God' in his daily life. He celebrates the *Pascha* of the Lord. All the feasts of the Church culminate in the Divine Liturgy, in *Pascha*, in a *Pascha* which can be celebrated every day by celebrating the Divine Liturgy as a daily Pascha.

Every celebration of the Divine Liturgy is a true and unrepeatable Pascha. Everything in the Liturgy happens for each individual in an unrepeatable way. At the same time, the Divine Liturgy is a constant repetition. It is a repetition of the unrepeatable Last Supper and the unrepeatable union of the believer with Christ. As with man's birth, so too his rebirth is a unique and unrepeatable act of repetition: the first on a physical, and the second on a spiritual level. The Liturgy is a work of God, and as a work of God it transcends time and belongs to eternity. Already the celebration of the Last Supper before the death on the Cross constitutes a reversal of historical time and a suspension of the normal temporal sequence.[32] Christ who offers himself as food and drink to his disciples, has not yet been crucified. And his disciples who receive the communion of the body and blood of Christ have not yet lived through the ordeal of his Death. The Last Supper actuates the sacrifice which, historically speaking, has not yet taken place.

---

[31]"It is not time that sets the hour for the celebration of the Liturgy, but the Liturgy that imposes itself on time." A. Kalyvopoulos, op.cit., p.90.

[32]See Archimandrite Sophrony, *Opsometha ton Theon kathos estin*, Essex, England 1992, p.360.

And the sacrifice of the Cross lays the foundations of the sacrament that, liturgically speaking, has already been instituted.

By taking part in the Divine Liturgy and approaching for Holy Communion, the believer experiences the unique and eternal event of his regeneration in Christ. Without ceasing to be in time, he nevertheless shares in eternity. Even one participation in Holy Communion would be sufficient for his regeneration. But since he is subject to the decay and deterioration which time inflicts, he comes 'again and often times' to the sacrament. But each one of these approaches is the one unrepeatable approach to the mystery of his union with Christ. It represents his approach to, and his progress within, the indestructible and constantly renewed communion which deifies the Church. Furthermore, whatever happens in time and is of truth, no longer belongs to time, but to eternity. And whatever is repeated in time and is of truth, is not confined to time but extends into eternity. Thus every Holy Eucharist is a repetition of the unique and unrepeatable Eucharist of the Last Supper.[33]

The Holy Eucharist, as the mystery (sacrament) that preserves the true life of the man of faith, is also the mystery which preserves his true memory: the memory of all the events in the divine economy, and of the events in the history of mankind in their eschatological perspective. In the mystery of the Holy Eucharist we have the greatest condensation of time. The present is joined to the past and the future, while the 'now' extends to a ceaseless 'ever.'

This condensation of time is clearly expressed in the Divine Liturgy that is celebrated in the Orthodox Church. Thus, in the prayer of the Anaphora in the Liturgy of St. Basil, the priest says: "Wherefore, we also, O Master, remember his saving Passion and life-giving Cross, his three days' Burial, and his Resurrection from the dead, his Ascension into heaven, and his Sitting on the Right Hand of thee, the God and Father, and his glorious and terrible Second Coming." Also, in the Liturgy of St. John Chrysostom, the priest says: "Remembering therefore

---

[33]"For by one offering he hath perfected forever them that are sanctified." Heb. 10:14.

this saving command, and all those things that were done for us: the Cross, the Tomb, the Resurrection on the third day, the Ascension into heaven, the Sitting at the Right Hand, the Second and glorious Coming again."

As is quite clear, liturgical memory here is not applied solely to the past, but also to the future. It does not present itself simply as remembrance of things that happened in time now lost, though the Church considers it won, but also as familiarization with things that are expected to happen.

What this liturgical condensation of time offers to the believer is not an emotional release from the restricting confines of the sensible world, but an existential transcendence with a view to, and in the name of, the transcendent presence of Christ. In this way, liturgical time with its commemorations of the events of divine economy, of the saints and of the Panagia, extends the building of the Body of Christ, i.e. the Church, into history. The entire lives of the faithful, and all their various efforts to respond to the call of God and keep his commandments, are bound up with the Divine Liturgy. All the failures and disappointments that occur in daily life and in the course of history look for their cure and restoration in the observance of the 'saving commandment' of the celebration of the Holy Eucharist. And it is the anxiety to respond to the commandments of God, and particularly to this saving commandment, that frees the believer from the tyranny of decay and death and leads him to taste of eternal life: "And I know that his commandment is life everlasting."[34]

This eternal life is not abstract or imaginary. It is God himself, who became man and manifested himself to the world in Christ. Faith in the God-man Christ, and acknowledgement of him as head of the Church make the transformation of time and participation in eternal life possible.

Man, who was created "in the image of God," preserves the character of his nature and the meaning of his existence as the springboard for his remembrance of God. But especially for a Christian, the memory of God is made concrete in the memory of Christ and his regenerative work in the world. So the con-

[34]John 12:50.

tent of the memory of Christ is the Church herself as the Body of Christ, the center and essence of which is the mystery of the Holy Eucharist.

St. Nicholas Cabasilas makes the observation that the entire economy which is in Christ is presented during the celebration of the Holy Eucharist in the bread, as though in a symbolic picture. Thus, we see in the bread Christ appearing as an infant, being led to his death, being crucified and having his side opened with the spear. Then we see the same bread being changed into the sacred Body of Christ, who in reality endured all these things and rose again and ascended into heaven and sits at the right hand of the Father.[35] Finally, just as the Holy Spirit descended after the conclusion of Christ's work, so the visitation of the Holy Spirit is proclaimed after the conclusion of the mystery of the Holy Eucharist.[36]

This summary review of all these events, which take place within an integral liturgical present that transcends time, is not some romantic concoction of the theologians and hymnographers of the Church, but is prescribed by the nature and provenance of the events themselves. Christ, who lived and acted in space and time as a historic person, is also at the same time the Lord of glory, "who is, and was, and is to come." He is the Lord of history, who does not remain beyond or outside time, but contains time and fills each moment of it. And the events in the life of Christ, just like all things that are associated with him and are recapitulated within his Body, sanctify and transform time. In this way, all time becomes sacred time. Every day and every moment is sanctified because it becomes a bearer of eternity. In the same way, all space becomes sacred because it is sanctified by spiritual worship.[37]

Thus, the mystery of the economy in Christ, which was accomplished once and for all in history, is celebrated in both microchronic and macrochronic cycles in the Church. It is concentrated into each day, yet also extends over the whole

---

[35]*Commentary on the Divine Liturgy* 37, PG150,452A.

[36]Nicholas Cabasilas, op. cit., PG150,452BC.

[37]"The hour cometh, when ye shall neither in this mountain, nor yet at Jerusalem, worship the Father . . . God is a Spirit," John 4:21-24.

year: now and forever. And the experience of this mystery in liturgical time is presented as extension into the future, which is accomplished by constant repetition. Every day, every week, every year, the same people and the same events are celebrated in a new way. The repetition of the same feast is at the same time a new feast, and participation in the same mystery is at the same time a new mystery. It is the experience of the same mystery in the always new and unique personal situation of each individual believer. Liturgical time unfolds as movement in a straight line, which is realized by a constant series of repetitions.

What the Church is to the world, liturgical time is to secular time. Just as in the Church the whole world is saved and transfigured, so in liturgical time all time is saved and transfigured. The world's time becomes the Church's time, and as the Church's time, it initiates the regeneration of all things.

Liturgical time transfigures physical time and transports us from symbol to truth, from the transient to the eternal, from creation to the Lord of creation. "For it certainly was not out of a wish that the days themselves be honored by men, that God ordained that the Sabbath and the first day of the month and the feast days be honored . . . but rather he suggested that these days be used as symbols to honor him."[38] Behind the symbols is the one symbolized. Behind the celebrations is the Lord who is celebrated. Christ is the Sabbath in the form of rest for mankind. He is the Pascha as deliverer of captives from sin. He is Pentecost as the beginning and end of existence. He is the cause and the goal of all things.[39] Thus, the function of time is to refer creation to the uncreated Creator. And man, who lives in time, knows God and is freed from the slavery of creation. He does not see time as the master of his life, but as a gift from the Master to him.

Finally, liturgical time is depicted in ecclesiastical iconography. But here too, time is not treated in its natural sequence, but condensed into a perpetual present. People who have lived

---

[38] Maximos the Confessor, *To Thalassios*, PG90,757B; *Various Chapters* 5,46, PG90,1368B.
[39] Op. cit.

at different periods in history, or events of no proximity to each other in time, are, as it were, synchronized and summarized in an eternal 'now.'[40] Included in this perspective is the depiction of founders and benefactors of churches next to saints or the Lord himself. But the most comprehensive and expressive manifestation of liturgical time lies in the liturgical life of the church itself. The Prophets, Apostles, Martyrs and Saints, the Panagia and the Lord the *Pantocrator* (the Almighty) depicted in the church, together with the congregation, represent a theanthropic communion, a divine-human communion which transcends the limitations of place and time.

---

[40]See K. Kalokyris, *I zografiki tis Orthodoxias*, Thessaloniki 1972, p. 207 ff.

Epilogue

Time is offered to man as a context for his dealings and encounters with his neighbor and with God. Time is also to be seen as the sphere wherein the love of God is revealed. It is in time that man encounters, or fails to encounter, God. It is in time that man shows, or fails to show, love for his neighbor. Finally, it is in time that he achieves, or fails to achieve, his correct orientation within the world around him. In the final analysis, man's correct orientation within the world is that which allows him to respond to God's love for him.

The means offered to man to respond to God's love consist of the three Christian virtues: faith, hope and love. With faith, man realizes God's love for him and he lives the beginnings of his own love for God and for his neighbor. With hope, he enjoys a foretaste of the love of God that awaits the world, which in turn encourages an increase in his own love. Finally, through the experience of the love of God in the present—which means, in fact, the mystical experience of that love in liturgical time—the believer passes beyond mere faith and hope. Thus, he responds to the love of God with his own personal love that, in imitation of the love of God, embraces the entire world.

The three fundamental Christian virtues thus correspond to the three dimensions of time: faith to the past, hope to the future, and love to the present. Just as the present in everyday life is seen as synthesis and transcendence of past and future, so too love emerges as synthesis and transcendence of man's faith and hope in God. Love, as a virtue of time present, is the bridge over which everything that the future has in store can be conveyed, so that it can then be placed in the past. Finally, love, like the present, is all that man has at his disposal as long as he lives in the world. Not only this, but it is also the only thing that will continue to exist when the world and time have come to an end.

Index

Adam, 42; (new Adam—see Christ).
adoption, 40, 47.
age, 6-10, 46; future age, 18, 53, 94.
aidion, (see also everlasting), 6-7, 45-46; and eternal, 7, 45-46.
anaphora, prayer of, 102.
Annunciation, 87, 95.
Antichrist, 52-53.
apostolic succession, 71.
apostolicity, 71-72;
Ascension, 44, 88, 94.

baptism, 36, 50, 52, 63, 91, 97.
bishop, 71-74.

catechumens, 91.
catholicity, 64.
celibacy, 72, 75-76.
child/children, 35, 60, 70, 93; spiritual, 70.
chrismation, 63, 97.
Christ, 5, 8, 30, 41-43, 67, 84-86, 97, 103-5; and history, 52-53; and time, 39, 40-41; and world, 40; as new Adam, 40, 42, 51, 90; Body of, 62-63, 101; Crucifixion of, 53, 54, 99, 101-102; death of, 5, 43, 84; divinity of, 86, 98; light of, 43, 47, 98; name of, 86; Passion of, 41; presence of, 40-41, 43, 51; renewing work of, 95, 103-104.
Christian, 72, 100; fatherland of, 22.
Christianity, 6, 62-64, 72; western, 66.
Christmas, 87, 95-97.
Church, 5, 18-21, 45, 51-52, 55-56, 59, 62, 95, 97, 103; and time, 5, 30, 51; and world, 20; as Body of Christ, 67, 71, 95, 103; head of, 83, 103; institutions, 55, 64, 73; members, 36, 74; Orthodox, 64-65, 68, 72, 90-91, 98, 102; unity of, 66, 71, 77.

civilization, 57.
clocks, 24-25; biological, 25.
commandment, 38, 90, 103.
communion, 51, 60-61, 66, 67-68, 81, 87; of deification, 55-56, 73, 74-75, 95, 102; with Christ, 50, 54, 68, 86-87; with God, 21, 36, 45, 52, 71-72, 76, 95.
Communion, Holy, 67, 72.
compline, 100.
conservatism, 62, 66, 68.
contentment, 17, 32.
creation, 5, 9, 40-42, 77, 99, 105.
created nature, 9, 46-47, 52.
Cross of Christ, 44, 78-79, 90-91, 92.
cycle, weekly, 87, 98-99; day and night offices, 100.

day, 58-59; eighth, 7, 99; last day, 48, 49, 51; judgement, 49 (see also Second Coming); liturgical, 99; of the Lord, 7, 45, 49, 58-59.
death, 15-16, 22, 24, 29-30, 32, 51-52, 57, 60, 68, 70, 75, 77, 81, 92, 100, 103-104; and life, 21, 28-29, 32, 92; and time, 20, 24; defeat of, 18, 20; fear of, 82; remembrance of, 29-30, 100; sovereignty over, 16, 21, 77.
decay, 4, 15-16, 51, 60, 64, 68, 77-78, 103.
deification, (see also theosis), 19, 30, 46-47, 97.
desire, 32, 42.
destruction, 15, 48, 58.
devil, 77, 90, 97.
divine energy, 43, 47.
Divine Liturgy, 54, 88, 101-102.

ecological crisis, 35.
economy, in Christ, 82, 104; divine, 17,

Index

44, 87, 94, 100-101, 102-103, 104; theandric, 63.
entropy, 29.
environment, 24, 32, 35, 64; environmental pollution, 35.
epitaphion, 93.
eros, 75.
eschata, 5, 33, 34, 50, 51-53, 68, 96.
eschatology, 1, 58; eschatological character, 5, 52; eschatological perspective, 68.
eternal, 10, 42, 45-46, 52; and everlasting, 6, 45-46; and temporality, 6, 42.
eternal life, participation in, 8, 82, 102.
eternity, 2, 4, 4-5, 11, 19, 36-37, 41, 42, 45, 46, 51, 55-56, 59, 65, 80-81, 98, 101-102, 105; and time, 2, 4, 6, 19, 56, 79-81; image of, 2, 80-81.
ethnicism, 20-21.
ethnic religion, 21.
Eucharist, Holy, 50, 54, 62-63, 65, 86, 92, 98-100, 102-104.
everlasting, (see aidion) 45-47, 56-57; and eternal, 7, 45-46; everlastingness, 45-47, 55-56.
evil, 97-97.
exodus, 16-18, 74.

faith, 5, 17, 67, 84, 86, 103.
fasting, 89-90, 91, 99.
fatherhood, spiritual, 71.
fear of death, 82.
feasts, 30, 86-88, 105; and the Resurrection, 93, 95, 98; immovable, 87, 95, 98; macrochronic, 89, 104; microchronic, 98, 104; moveable, 87-88, 95, 98; of the Lord, 87, of the Panagia, 95, 97; of saints, 95, 98.
freedom, 15-16, 20, 75, 81, 95, 96; in Christ, 22, 91.
future, 2, 6, 11-13, 23-24, 27, 30-31, 34-35, 51, 59, 66, 79-80, 81-82, 85, 102.

God, 5, 7, 9, 45, 58, 98-99; as eternal, 10, 45, 52, 97; as everlasting, 10, 45; as timeless, 7, 39, 96; likeness towards, 30; will of, 55-56, 96; glory of, 45, 50, 52, 85, 86, 98.

God-man, 41, 85, 86, 103; love of, 19, 55, 57; knowledge of, 48; revelation of, 19, 21, 39-40.
grace, uncreated, 9, 42, 47, 52.

hell, 27.
history, 5, 21-22, 39, 40, 45, 51, 53, 55-57, 67, 81, 88, 97, 101, 102-103, 104-105, 105-106; and eschatology, 57; of civilization, 57; and Old Testament, 19, 40, 94; meaning of, 21-22.
Holy Land, 17.
Holy Spirit, (see also Paraclete), 8, 19, 44-45, 51-52, 63-64, 67, 76, 94-95, 97, 104; fruits of, 41; grace of, 21, 63-64, 67, 97.
Holy Trinity, 97.
Holy Week, 91, 92, 99.
Holy Unction, 92.
homoousios, 65.
hope, 16-17, 24, 30, 66, 81, 84, 86.
hours, 100-101.
humility, 89, 90-91.

iconography, 105.
idolatry, 20, 21.
immortality, 45.
Incarnation, 40, 44, 48, 96.
individualism, 61.
industrial revolution, 31.
intellect, 12, 13, 27, 42, 80.
intelligible, 4, 9.
intercessions, 87.

joy, 17, 24, 29, 58, 94.

kairos, 4, 36, 38, 46, 52, 58, 81, 87.
kingdom of God, 18, 22, 47-48, 52, 68, 74, 79, 82, 86, 87; revelation of the, 51-52, 55-56, 87; symbol of, 18, 68.

Last Supper, (see Mystical Supper).
Lent, Great, 89, 90-91, 99.
life, 8, 16, 23, 51, 60, 66, 70, 92, 103, 105; and death, 21, 29-30, 32, 92; eternal, 5, 18, 38, 41, 46, 54, 57, 103; future, 7, 10, 79, 84; in Christ, 65, 78-79, 80, 83, 85-86; monastic, 73, 76; of the faithful, 54, 83, 84, 103, 105;

present, 9-10, 57, 79, 84; purpose of, 34, 46; spiritual, 30, 73, 74, 76; true, 57, 92, 102; way of, 35, 61.
light, 47, 86; of Christ, (see Christ); divine, 47, 50; of the Transfiguration, 53; true, 100; uncreated, 47, 53-54.
likeness, 42; of God, 30.
Liturgy, Divine, 54, 88, 101-102.
liturgical year, 88.
Lord's day, the, 7, 45, 49, 58-59.
love, 67, 89, 91, 93; of God (see God); of self, 97.

man, 25, 28, 30, 33-34, 41-42, 46-47, 48, 52, 77, 92, 103; and God, 10, 42, 46-47, 52; as eternal, 46-47; as everlasting, 46-47, 52; as created in the image and likeness of God, 42, 81, 99; as unoriginate, 46-47; and archetype, 42; and disorientation, 32; and knowledge, 32; nature of, 23, 30, 44, 46, 52; as organism, 25-26.
marriage, 74-76; as spiritual, 72, 74-75, 76, 91.
matter, 43, 98.
memory, (also remembrance), 23, 27, 61, 82; liturgical, 102; of death, 30; eternal, 92.
Messiah, 19, 52.
metanoia, (see repentance).
midnight office, 100.
millennialism, 20.
monastery, 70, 72-73.
monasticism, 64, 70, 72-73, 74.
monk, 22, 61, 70.
monotheism, 20.
movement, 2, 12, 15.
mystery, 59, 62-63, 83, 99, 102, 104, 105; of Christ's presence, 59, 62; of Church, 62; of Priesthood, 71.
Mystical Supper, (also Last Supper), 92, 101-102.
mythology, 23, 41.
mutability, 30, 46, 77, 81.

nature, 42; created, 8, 42, 47; uncreated, 8.

now, 2, 45, 85.

pain, 27, 58.
Panagia (see Theotokos).
Paraclete (see Holy Spirit).
paradise, 89-90.
parents, 35, 60, 61; spiritual parents, 70.
participation, in eternal life, 54; in life in Christ, 83; in divine life, 8.
Pascha, 88, 93-94, 98, 101, 105.
passions, passion, 30.
'passionless-hatred', 70.
past, 2, 6, 11-12, 13, 23, 25, 27, 30, 59, 66-67, 80, 81-83, 85, 102.
peace, 37.
Pentecost, 52, 53, 88, 94-95, 105.
Pentecostarion, 93.
perfection, 30, 36-37, 77-78, 83, 96.
philanthropy, 55, 89.
place, 18, 22, 61.
political changes, 31-32.
pollution, environmental, 35.
polytheism, 20.
prayer of Anaphora, 102.
present, 2, 6, 11, 13, 23, 27, 30, 35, 51, 66-67, 79-81, 82, 84-85, 102.
progress, 58; spiritual, 70.
promised land, 18, 91.
prostration, 55.
purity, 30, 76; of heart, 26, 30, 85.

relativity, 28.
remembrance, 12, 27; of death, 29-30, 100; of God, 103.
renewal, 36-37, 44, 51, 77-78, 103; of the world, 20, 44, 99.
repentance, 27, 37, 83.
resurrection, 5, 17, 41, 44, 52-54, 93, 95, 99-100.
righteousness, 49, 85.

saints, 44, 52, 53, 73-74, 79-80, 84, 95-96, 98; feast days of (see feasts).
salvation, 77, 81, 91.
Saturday, 99, 105.
Saturday of Souls, 89, 94.

Index

science, 14, 31, 32, 34.
Second Coming, 12-13, 47, 49, 89, 100.
secularization, 4, 64, 74.
selfishness, 61.
sensible, 4, 9, 79.
sermon, 63, 63, 64.
services, 87, 98.
sin, 37, 55, 77, 84, 90, 92.
slavery, 40, 89.
soul, 4, 26-27.
space, 2, 5-6, 12-14, 15, 33, 36, 50, 58, 61, 67, 104; sacred, 17-18, 19, 104; transcendence of, 18-19.
Spirit, Holy, 8, 19.
spiritual children, 70.
spiritual fatherhood, 71.
spiritual experience, 47, 73.
spiritual 'trade', 37-38.
spiritual warfare, 83, 97.
spiritual worship, 104.
Sunday, 88, 90, 98-99; of the Veneration of the Holy Cross, 90.
symbol, 18, 47, 53-54, 68, 71, 86, 93, 105.

technology, 31, 32, 34.
temple, 17-18, 52, 106.
temporal, 7, 42.
temporality, 26, 46-47, 54, 85, 88.
theology, 7, 53.
Theophany, 95, 97.
theory of relativity, 13.
theosis, (see deification).
Theotokos, (also Panagia), 40, 42-43, 43, 72-73, 87, 95, 96, 97, 103.
time, 1, 12-14, 16, 20, 24, 25-26, 27-28, 34, 35-36, 41-43, 44-45, 50, 51, 58-59, 67, 80-81, 103, 104; absolute, 4, 13, 39; and dreams, 26; and events, 5, 14, 27, 41, 52, 102, 105-106; and world, 6,9; as spiral, 6; beginning of, 1, 6, 40, 49-56; biblical, 4; Church, 5, 83, 103; cyclical, 1, 16; experience of, 14, 33-34; fullness of, 39; internal, 26; inversion of, 42; limitations of, 16, 57; linear concept of, 6, 24, 55, 57; liturgical, 88, 102-103, 104-106; Lord of, 5, 58; measurement of, 12; momentum of, 6, 24-25, 29, 42, 66; mythical, 41; nature of, 1, 2-3, 6, 25, 33, 48; objectivization of, 24; physical, 25; psychic, 27-28; recycling of, 1, 16; renewal of, 45; sacred, 41, 104; sanctification of, 87; the end of, 1, 6, 40, 49, 56; view of, 1-2, 5-6, 12-13, 34, 45, 67.
'time-space', 13.
tomb of Christ, 44, 78.
tonsure, 70.
tradition, 60, 76; biblical, 13, 43; of Fathers, 10, 43, 46, 48, 67, 68.
traditionality, 62, 65.
transcendence, of time, 54; of space, 18-19.
transfiguration, 52, 53, 103; of man, 19, 77-78; of place, 22; of the past, 83; of time, 77, 83-84, 88; of world, 77.
Transfiguration, light of, 53 (see also light).
Triodion, 88, 89.
Truth, 76, 78-79, 85-86, 77.

uncreated, 52.
Unction, Holy, 92.
universe, 12, 14, 48; renewal of, 41; end of, 48.

vespers, 58, 93, 100.
virginity, 72, 74-76, 96.
virtue, 82, 84, 97.

warfare, spiritual, 83, 97.
way of life, 18, 34, 61.
week, 98-99.
weekly cycle, 87, 98-99.
world, 6-7, 12-13, 22, 38, 41, 55-56, 59, 63-64, 74, 77, 105; beginning of, 5; creation of, (see creation); end of, 5, 48-49, 56; renewal of (see renewal); salvation of, 51; transcendence of, 18, 64; transfiguration of, 77-78.